— UNDERSTANDING *the* —
CONSTITUTION

"Our Constitution was made only

for a moral and religious people.

It is wholly inadequate to the

government of any other."

John Adams,
President of the United States, 1797-1801

Published by the National Center for Life and Liberty
P.O. Box 270548, Flower Mound, Texas 75027-0548
Telephone: 888.233.NCLL (6255)
www.ncll.org

Printed in the United States of America.

Contents

Introduction

The United States Constitution is the legal blueprint by which our American government is to operate. It is intended to be the guarantor of our liberties, but it is not the grantor of those liberties.

Many Americans have never once read this short document completely through, and most have erroneous views of what it says. One survey found that 36% of Americans are unable to identify any one of the five rights guaranteed by the First Amendment (freedom of speech, religion, press, assembly and petition for redress of grievances).[1] Another survey showed that only 28% could name two of those five freedoms, while just one American in 1,000 (one-tenth of one percent) could name all five.[2]

When given the list of possible rights from which to choose, those surveyed did not do much better. One in five thought the right to own a pet was a protected First Amendment right! More than 1/3 also believed that the right against self-incrimination was in the First Amendment [3] (it is in the Bill of Rights, but in the Fifth Amendment, not the First). These appalling results demonstrate a tragically widespread ignorance among our citizens of America's most basic fundamental freedoms.

This book is not intended to be a detailed legal analysis of the Constitution. It is intended to be a basic introduction to this most important of American documents, concentrating primarily on those constitutional provisions that affect religious liberty. For example, many Americans today, including some Christians, believe that the Constitution requires the separation of church and state; yet, these words never appear in either the Constitution or any of its amendments.

Every American should be aware of what the Constitution actually says. Americans, however, should also heed the warning of John Adams, our second president and a signer of the Declaration of Independence, that America as a nation can never be saved by the Constitution alone; rather, we must also continue to heed the timeless principles that undergird it.[4]

All Americans, of every faith and of no faith, need to understand what is at stake today in our nation. Since the 1960s, because of various decisions by the United States Supreme Court favoring secularism over religion, America has begun to stray from its founding biblical principles. Some Americans seem to want to forget God, the Grantor of our rights. We regularly disregard His laws and no longer think them important to our survival as a nation. Courts have jettisoned major portions of our Judeo-Christian heritage as unconstitutional.

John Adams warned us, his posterity, that Christian virtue is an implied assumption of our constitutional form of government, in writing to his Massachusetts constituents on October 11, 1798:

> [W]e have no government armed with power capable of contending with human passions unbridled by morality and religion. Avarice, ambition, revenge, or gallantry, would break the strongest cords of our Constitution as a whale goes through a net. Our Constitution was made only for a moral and religious people. It is wholly inadequate to the government of any other.[5]

America, like every nation on the face of the earth, can only avoid God's judgment if we heed the call of II Chronicles 7:14: *"If my people, which are called by my name, shall humble themselves, and pray, and seek my face, and turn from their wicked ways; then will I hear from heaven, and will forgive their sin, and will heal their land."*

The Bible tells us that citizens of every nation have a duty to obey their government. Christians also have a special biblical duty to pray for their governmental leaders. I Timothy 2:1-4 says:

> I exhort therefore, that, first of all, supplications, prayers, intercessions, and giving of thanks, be made for all men; For kings, and for all that are in authority; that we may lead a quiet and peaceable life in all godliness and honesty. For this is good and acceptable in the sight of God our Saviour; Who will have all men to be saved, and to come unto the knowledge of the truth.

This passage of Scripture explains *why* we should pray. Our knowledge of our protected constitutional rights and duties will guide us in *what* we should pray.

Good Christians should always be good citizens and, therefore, should become very familiar with the laws of our nation. We are commanded in Scripture to obey the law. The Bible commands us to *"be subject unto the higher powers."* (Romans 13:1) In fact, I Peter 2:13-16 makes it quite clear that our submission to government is the will of God and an important aspect of our testimony:

> *Submit yourselves to every ordinance of man for the Lord's sake: whether it be to the king, as supreme; Or unto governors, as unto them that are sent by him for the punishment of evildoers, and for the praise of them that do well. For so is the will of God, that with well doing ye may put to silence the ignorance of foolish men: As free, and not using your liberty for a cloke of maliciousness, but as the servants of God.*

Yet, how can Christians, or any citizens, obey the law or participate fully in our government if we do not know what the law actually says? This book is intended for all Americans, but it is especially intended to be a challenge and an encouragement for American Christians to learn more about the Constitution and its protection of our religious liberties.

The time may come when the religious liberties with which the Lord has blessed our nation will no longer exist in America, and Christians will be forced to decide whether to obey their government or to obey their God. Choosing to disobey government should always be a last resort, however, taken only after every attempt to reconcile man's law with God's law has failed.

The best guarantee that our constitutional freedoms will continue to be protected in America is to make certain that all citizens clearly understand both what those freedoms are and Who it is that has granted Americans those freedoms. Our Founders recognized in the Declaration of Independence that it is not government, but the Judeo-Christian God of the Bible Who is the sole Grantor of freedom. Governments are instituted by men, our Declaration of Independence proclaims, merely to recognize and protect the freedoms that have already been given to every person on the face of the earth by God Almighty, the Creator God of the Bible, the One who was recognized as Creator and Grantor of liberty by all of America's Founders.

Chapter 1

America's Legal Foundation

Although America's Constitution was originally based
on principles grounded in the law of nature and nature's
God, secular interests have eroded that foundation.

Beginning in the 1600s, America, as a group of independent colonies and then later as a united nation, has experienced more than 400 years of Divine blessing in a society that has produced the greatest degree of freedom ever known in the history of the world. From its inception, America's legal system was based on the Bible and on British common law principles that derived from the eternal and immutable Law of the Creator, articulated best in 1765 by William Blackstone in his *Commentaries on the Laws of England*. These common law principles were enshrined a decade later in the Declaration of Independence (1776) and in America's Constitution (1787).

America's Constitution has changed very little in the more than 200 years since it was written. Our nation, however, has changed a great deal since then. As societal changes have escalated, primarily since the mid-20th century, judges have adapted the meaning of the Constitution to "keep up with the times." The question to be considered is whether those changes have been good or bad for America.

Generations of Americans who have grown up since the start of the 20th century, generally speaking, have absolutely no idea about the founding religious heritage of their country. Indeed, most Americans today do not know that the very foundation of our nation's Constitution and legal system was built on the principles of the Bible.

The biblical principles upon which our Declaration of Independence and Constitution are based were adapted from British common law, which consisted generally of unwritten laws and customs developed over time in England. This common law derived from both natural law and God's revealed law in the Bible, and was recognized in the English Magna Carta of 1215, when nobles challenged the king with the concept that he was not the highest ruler in the land. God himself was the highest ruler, and the king must rule subject to God's law first. America's Founders recognized these common law biblical principles as being foundational to liberty and enshrined them in our Declaration when it refers to the rights to which "the laws of nature and of nature's God" entitle us.

Later, William Blackstone wrote down these principles of the common law in his *Commentaries*, published in 1765, a decade before America's Revolutionary War. The *Commentaries* also pointed out the flaws that had developed over time in British law. Interestingly, these books enjoyed greater popularity in the colonies just before the Revolutionary War than they did in England.

Blackstone's *Commentaries* provided a written, legal foundation for the new nation of America—a foundation that was represented in the Declaration of Independence and the Constitution. While the Americanized, written common law system established a separation between the jurisdictions of church and state, it nevertheless firmly placed both of these jurisdictions under God—just as the nobles had done in 1215 in England when they confronted the king.

John C.H. Wu has explained the history of the common law in modern times in his book, *"Fountain of Justice."*[1] Wu concludes that *"the common law was Christian from the very beginning,"* and that *"it gradually assimilated the principles of natural law, not as an abstract theory, but as vital practical rules of human conduct."*[2] Joseph Story, Associate Justice of the Supreme Court from 1811-1845 was an early expositor of the common law in America. In his 1829 inaugural discourse as a professor of law at Harvard University, Justice Story said, *"One of the beautiful boasts of our municipal jurisprudence is that Christianity is a part of the common law."* He continued, *"There never has been a period in which the Common Law did not recognize Christianity as lying at its foundations."*[3]

Beginning at the end of the Civil War in the mid-19th century, and escalating in the mid-20th century, however, America began to gradually move away from these common law principles. Law schools began to teach a different type of law to their students in the early 20th century and by the mid-20th century the legal landscape had changed significantly in America.

In 1990, Attorney David Gibbs III attended one of his first classes as a first-year law student at Duke University School of Law. The professor in whose class he sat had clerked at the highest levels of America's federal courts, including serving as clerk for two different Supreme Court Justices. He also had an impressive career in the private practice of law, but had dedicated himself, while still a young man, to teaching future lawyers as a constitutional law professor at Duke. This was his opening lecture, one that was more philosophical in nature, but one that he deemed to be the most important.

As the professor began the class, he stated that what he was about to tell the students was the most important change in the law that had happened during his lifetime, and while the students would not recognize it now, this change would greatly impact the legal careers of every future lawyer.

He told the class that while they might not fully understand what he was about to say, they should be sure to write it all down because it was very important. All the students prepared to write. This was certainly going to be on a test at some point!

The professor declared that the biggest change to have occurred in American law was the fact that the common law was now dead in America.

At that time, this class of legal "newbies" had no idea what he was talking about. The only common law most of them had ever heard about was "common law marriage" where people could become married in the eyes of the law if they had lived together out of wedlock for a long enough period of time. The students imagined that since so many people were now living together out of wedlock that must mean these legally imposed marriages were no longer necessary. The professor interrupted their thoughts and continued:

> We now live in the era of statutory law, not common law. That is the largest change in jurisprudence since America was founded as a nation. It has happened in my lifetime, and while you may not fully understand what I am saying—remember this—it will impact your lives, your families, and your future practice of law. The common law is now dead in America.

It wasn't until a few years into their law school process that the students began to see the full import of what their professor had said. By telling the class that common law was now dead in America, the professor was letting the students know that any absolute standard in the law—i.e., any Divine standard for law, had now been replaced by man-centered statutory law. By recognizing this, the professor was letting his class know that the law is no longer something that is "fixed, uniform, and universal" at all times and in all places, as William Blackstone wrote and as America's Founders had believed. Instead, statutory law is a man-made law based on what 51% of those voting can agree on in any given court, legislative body or public referendum. In biblical terms from the Book of Judges, we could say that statutory law is essentially men *"doing what is right in their own eyes."*

Years ago, men would do what they thought to be right according to the common law —the standard found in the Word of God. Now this Duke law professor must let every class of law students in on the secret—that America no longer has any definite standards for the law. Whatever men think is best now takes on fancy terms like "meeting societal needs" and "determining good public policy," but the truth is clear. The Bible no longer sets the standard for American law. Legislators and judges now write the laws, determine the policies, and decide the cases based on what they think is best for America—their own personal preferences.

This professor's declaration has taken on an even more dramatic impact as Attorney Gibbs and other lawyers have watched the law unfold during their legal careers. A whole generation of adults has now been educated in public schools where prayer and Bible reading have been declared illegal. A whole generation of adults has watched abortion consume the lives of more than fifty-five million unborn babies in America. A whole generation of adults has watched sexual immorality come out of the closet, become non-criminal, move into being a fashionable special interest group, and is now on the way to becoming a constitutionally protected category demanding all the rights and privileges of marriage, adoption, and other legal benefits and privileges traditionally preserved for God-ordained marriage under the common law (one man/one woman). This secularist-educated generation now sits on our courts, on juries, and in our legislatures making decisions based not on God's law, but on what they think is best for America. These new secularists have little or no connection with America's foundational Judeo-Christian heritage established in the Declaration of Independence and the Constitution. No wonder America is teetering on the brink of disaster.

America was founded as a nation by religious men who understood biblical truth and principles. These Judeo-Christian principles motivated and controlled their decisions. The America they founded, under God, is now having its future shaped and its past re-characterized by judges who are unfamiliar with the Bible, who are uncomfortable with organized religion, and who are unwilling to be controlled by any higher authority or principle beyond their own minds. Their thoughts, feelings, and emotions on any given issue control their decisions because there is no absolute truth they feel obligated to respect as a controlling authority in their lives.

Particularly in the last few decades, the Constitution has taken on vastly different interpretations and applications from what was originally intended. The following legal principles now play integral roles in how American law is being shaped: the practice of judicial review; judges and Supreme Court Justices who take a liberal/progressive interpretation of the Constitution; expansion of the Bill of Rights to the states via the Fourteenth Amendment; massive growth of federal power under the Commerce Clause; and a Darwinian-inspired evolutionary approach to case law. The following sections will discuss how each of these principles and practices has grown the power of the federal government to become what was never even remotely considered by the men who created our founding documents.

I. JUDICIAL REVIEW

The concept of "judicial review" has shaped American jurisprudence like no other. The term itself is not found in the Constitution. Section 2 of Article III lists the enumerated powers of the Supreme Court:

> *Section 2. The judicial Power shall extend to all Cases, in Law and Equity, arising under this Constitution, the Laws of the United States, and Treaties made, or which shall be made, under their Authority; - to all Cases affecting Ambassadors, other public Ministers and Counsels; - to all cases of admiralty and maritime Jurisdiction; - to Controversies to which the United States shall be a Party; - to Controversies between two or more States; - between a State and Citizens of another State; - between Citizens of different States, - between Citizens of the same State claiming Lands under Grants of different States, and between a State, or the Citizens thereof and foreign States, Citizens or Subjects.*

In spite of its noticeable absence in the Constitution, the judicial review doctrine has been used to some extent by judges almost from the beginning of our Republic. It is under the doctrine of judicial review that the Supreme Court has given constitutional protection to freedoms and rights that were not specifically enumerated therein. In short, judicial review has permitted the Justices of the Supreme Court to impose their own biases, prejudices, and desires on the rest of the nation under the guise of constitutional interpretation.

The Supreme Court first asserted its right to judicial review of all actions taken by the other branches of government in the case of *Marbury* v. *Madison*, 5 U.S. 137 (1803). This was the most famous, or infamous, decision handed down by the Marshall Court, and it was important for at least two reasons. First, the Court marked new territory for itself by asserting it had a judicial power to review the acts of other branches of the federal government. Additionally, this case signified the first time the Supreme Court declared an act of Congress to be unconstitutional. This would only happen one other time before the Civil War.

Even though today few would argue that the Court does not have the power of judicial review, such was not the case when Chief Justice John Marshall authored the *Marbury* decision. However, after this landmark decision, the assertion that the Supreme Court had the authority to interpret the Constitution and to void the acts of other branches of government on this basis was rapidly accepted. This decision established the Supreme Court as the supreme keeper of the Constitution to the exclusion of the executive and legislative branches of our government.

In a series of cases beginning in 1803, when *Marbury* was decided, until 1821, the Court granted to itself these powers...

- Power to review the acts of other branches of the federal government, and the authority to declare such acts unconstitutional (*Marbury* v. *Madison*, 5 U.S. 137 (1803))

- Power to invalidate a state law under the Constitution (*Fletcher* v. *Peck*, 10 U.S. 87 (1810))

- Authority to be the single, final interpreter of federal law and the Constitution (*Martin* v. *Hunter's Lessee*, 14 U.S. 304 (1816)); and

- Authority to review state criminal proceedings (*Cohens* v. *Virginia*, 19 U.S. 264 (1821)).

Thus, the stage was set for a radical future expansion of the Constitution by the judiciary, an unelected body.

II. PHILOSOPHICAL EXPANSION OF THE CONSTITUTION

Judges generally use one of three philosophical methods to interpret the U. S. Constitution:

1. **Strict construction**, which interprets the document to mean exactly what it states and nothing more or less.

2. **Historical approach**, which interprets the Constitution by analyzing its history and what was meant at the time of its writing.

3. **Liberal (or Progressive) approach**, which views the Constitution as a "living document" in the sense that its words and phrases must be interpreted in light of our modern desires and the needs of our modern society and not according to the intent of its authors.

Today, a majority of lower court judges and Supreme Court Justices use the liberal/progressive approach to deciding cases. Only a small minority use the strict construction or historical approach to interpret the Constitution. This departure from the original intent of our Constitution's Founders has given rise over the years to a greatly expanded interpretation of federal government power under the Constitution and to vast changes in our nation's laws.

III. EXPANSION UNDER THE FOURTEENTH AMENDMENT

The Fourteenth Amendment has been another primary method by which the power of the federal government has been expanded. Until this Amendment was ratified, the guarantees under the Bill of Rights were only applicable against infringements of citizens' rights by the federal government, not by the states. States protected the fundamental rights of their own citizens through their own individual state constitutions and courts. Since the Bill of Rights was originally written for the purpose of protecting the people from the federal government, the states were free to individually determine which of their citizens' rights they would protect. This fact was recognized by the Supreme Court prior to the Civil War in *Barron v. Mayor and City Council of Baltimore*, 32 U.S. 243 (1833).

Following the Civil war, however, the federal government began to assume more power over actions of the states with regard to citizens' rights. The Fourteenth Amendment was ratified in 1868 to guarantee that the newly freed slaves in the South would be treated by their state governments in the same way as all other citizens in the state. The Amendment guaranteed that no state *"shall make or enforce any law which shall abridge the privileges or immunities of citizens of the United States; nor shall any State deprive any person of life, liberty, or property, without due process of law."* This amendment was never intended to extend all of the individual rights protected by the Bill of Rights to the individual states.

Today, however, the Supreme Court has ruled that all the rights it deems to be essential or fundamental to the American system of justice are now applicable to actions by states and localities by incorporation through the Fourteenth Amendment. This has given the federal government increasing power over state and local governments, something the original Constitution did not anticipate.

IV. EXPANSION UNDER THE COMMERCE CLAUSE

In Article I, section VIII of the Constitution, the Congress is granted power to regulate commerce between the states. The Supreme Court has expanded interpretation of this "Commerce Clause" to vastly enlarge the powers of the federal government. These federal powers now include areas once controlled solely by individual states. Beginning in 1937, with President Franklin D. Roosevelt's New Deal, the Supreme Court took an entirely different and much broader approach to interpreting the Clause. After 1937, governmental power gradually moved toward the federal government and away from the states, despite the fact that the Tenth Amendment had previously reserved to the states and individuals those powers not specifically granted to the federal government in the Constitution.

As a result, Congress, with the Supreme Court's blessing, now has relatively unfettered power to regulate areas of law that were never intended to be controlled by the federal government. The key United States Supreme Court case that strengthened the view of the Commerce Clause, and thus weakened the Tenth Amendment, was the 1937 case of *NLRB* v. *Jones & McLaughlin Steel Corp.*, 301 U.S. 1 (1937). After FDR unsuccessfully threatened to pack the Court by expanding it from nine to fifteen Justices, the Court, nevertheless, began to declare FDR's New Deal legislation to be constitutional using an expanded view of the Commerce Clause. The Court ruled that the Commerce Clause could be used to enable the federal government to regulate state as well as federal activity if the state activity had a "substantial economic effect" on interstate commerce or the "cumulative effect" of such state activities substantially affected interstate commerce.

That principle soon led to the federal government being constitutionally permitted, under the Commerce Clause, to regulate even what local farmers were permitted to grow on their own land for use on their own table. In the case of *Wicard* v. *Filburn*, 317 U.S. 111 (1942), the Court ruled that Mr. Filburn was not constitutionally permitted to plant and eat his own wheat because that activity violated the New Deal's Agricultural Adjustment Act. That Act limited farmers to planting 11.1 acres of wheat. Mr. Filburn was criminally charged for planting 23 acres to use for his own consumption. The Court held that Filburn's activities in the aggregate would have a substantial effect on interstate commerce since farmers could avoid purchasing wheat if they were permitted to grow it only for their own use.

These changes in the Court's view of the Commerce Clause have since then greatly affected three areas of law: civil rights legislation, federal criminal laws concerning traditionally state and local crimes, and the regulation of activities of state governmental entities.

For example, the Supreme Court invoked the power of the Commerce Clause to uphold the constitutionality of Title VII of the Civil Rights Act of 1964, which imposed federal penalties on anyone who deprived another person of equal enjoyment of places of public accommodation on the basis of race, color, religion or national origin. In the cases of *Heart of Atlanta Motel* v. *U.S.*, 379 U.S. 241 (1964) and *Katzenbach* v. *McClung*, 379 U.S. 274 (1964), the Court found that two small businesses fell within the reach of the Commerce Clause and could thus be subject to Title VII (a federal law) prohibiting racial discrimination: the Heart of Atlanta motel, because it served interstate travelers, and the restaurant in *Katzenbach*, because it served food that had crossed state lines, even though the customers were local.

The Commerce Clause, used in 1964 to end the sins of segregation and racial discrimination, has now become a mechanism for expanding the power of the federal government into countless other areas. Under the Commerce Clause, Congress and the federal government have gained unlimited power to regulate both civil and criminal activity even in areas once reserved to the states under the Tenth Amendment.

V. EXPANSION UNDER THE APPLICATION
OF EVOLUTIONARY PRINCIPLES

In 1859, nearly one hundred years after the publication of William Blackstone's *Commentaries on the Laws of England* (1765), Charles Darwin published his revolutionary book, *The Origin of Species*. While ostensibly a book about biological evolution, philosophical and legal scholars seized on the general theory of evolution as a way to eliminate America's legal dependence on the Creator God of the Bible Who was credited in the Declaration of Independence with bestowing natural rights on all humanity. Darwin's theory of evolution provided a legal and philosophical, as well as a biological, anchor that could be used to reinterpret life without the need for a Creator Who had the authority to impose His will on His created subjects. That was exactly what some of America's leading jurists were looking for in the late 19th century. These jurists wanted to reserve for themselves the right to determine what laws should regulate life on earth.

Oliver Wendell Holmes, Jr., lauded as a great legal philosopher and jurist of that time, was one of those jurists seeking a way to free mankind from the legal constraints imposed by a Creator. Holmes began arguing in his 1881 book, *The Common Law*, that the only source of law, properly speaking, is a judicial decision enforced by the State. In other words, judges, not God, should say what the law is. Holmes and other leading jurists and legal scholars argued throughout the second half of the 19th century for a radical new approach to the law, a legal system in which judges would not discover Divine law, as was previously assumed under common law principles, but would actually formulate the law themselves by evolving it, case by case, over time. Judges would then be free to move the law in any direction they determined would improve a progressive and evolving society.

Both of these beliefs—the belief in evolution, not Creation; and the belief in Man, not God—have dominated the teaching of law since the early part of the 20th century. Before 1900, American lawyers studied the law primarily by reading William Blackstone's books on the common law. The first 140 pages of Blackstone's *Commentaries* outline the biblical precepts and principles that controlled English common law. The remainder of the *Commentaries* describes how this law was being interpreted (not always correctly) in England. For the first hundred years of its existence, America's Founders and, later, its judges and lawyers, used Blackstone's common law principles to develop a legal system for the newly emerging nation.

Around 1900, however, buttressed by Darwin's new biological theories,

Dean Christopher Columbus Langdell at the new Harvard Law School deliberately substituted evolutionary legal principles for the fixed, uniform, and universal laws of God, which the common law and Blackstone's Commentaries had previously enshrined in American jurisprudence. The idea that man was no longer subordinate to God in the legal arena was widely hailed as a new, modern, legal theory destined to leave behind the religious constraints of the past.

As an Associate Justice of the United States Supreme Court in 1917, Oliver Wendell Holmes, Jr. wrote a dissenting opinion in which he proclaimed America's independence from Divine law and the nation's right to determine its own law without God. He boldly declared:

> *The common law is not a brooding omnipresence in the sky [based on God], but the articulate voice of some [earthly] sovereign, or quasi sovereign that can be identified.*

So. Pacific Co. v. *Jensen*, 244 U.S. 205, 222 (1917) (Oliver Wendell Holmes Jr., dissenting).

Supreme Court Chief Justice Charles Evans Hughes also reflected this early 20th century trend when he proclaimed in a 1907 speech: "We are under a Constitution, but the Constitution is what the judges say it is."[4]

These elite legal thinkers, intent on undermining the authority of God in American law, abandoned the biblical principles memorialized in Blackstone's *Commentaries*, the Declaration of Independence, the common law, and the Constitution. As lawyers began to attend law schools that ignored Blackstone and taught a far-reaching legal theory of evolving case precedents, the law was permitted to expand and grow into whatever shape secular jurists desired.

After this deliberate move away from God, American jurisprudence coasted for quite some time on the collective biblical memory of the past. But this memory became increasingly faded and jaded. In the 1960s, American culture began to join the chorus of these legal philosophers and, since then, the God of the Bible Who guided and inspired the Founders has been gradually pushed almost entirely out of America's legal system.

VI. A DISCONNECTED GENERATION

Whole generations of Americans growing up today have absolutely no idea that the heritage of this nation is based on the Bible. Even many older adults, who grew up under a different educational system, have become convinced that America was founded by a group of "separationists" whose primary goal was to create an environment where all public places like schools, courts, and government buildings would be "religion-free zones." Many Americans today live as if they really believe that the Founding Fathers intended for us to experience both liberty and licentiousness. Many have been led to believe that our Founders would be comfortable with the moral filth and unrighteousness we now live with every day in America. Sometimes it seems that any idea may be expressed in America today except the truth of the Gospel of Jesus Christ.

During the 1960s, the philosophical worldview of postmodernism[1], which at its core denies the possibility of any absolute truth, became dominant in American higher education, just as it was also beginning to dominate the courts. This radical worldview had previously been confined almost exclusively to intellectual circles; however, like the good Darwinians they were, a relative handful of philosophical activists, secularist academicians, and judges succeeded in moving the American legal system away from God towards a legal system in which truth is what the judges say it is. This shift in philosophy and worldview took place over the course of about ninety years—from the post-Civil War period in the 1870s, when the new legal system was beginning to be suggested by Oliver Wendell Holmes Jr., until the 1960s, when the evolving case law method based on Darwin's ideology, began to be fully implemented by the courts.

As a result, the American legal system has undergone a significant change as the United States Supreme Court, using this evolving case method approach, has taken a decidedly more hostile view of religion, and especially of biblical Christianity, the bulwark of the Constitution. This hostility is based on the postmodern presupposition that truth is relative for each person (i.e; there is no absolute truth by which we can guide our lives, either as individuals or as a nation). This is a monumental change from the attitude of our Founding Fathers, who initially based America's government and the rights of its citizens on the absolute sovereignty of God and the absolute truth of the Bible.

---

[1] Postmodernism is a late 20th century Western movement, characterized by a skeptical relativism and a general suspicion of "modern" reason. It denies the existence of ultimate truth or principles and stands against the existence of any unifying scientific, philosophical, or religious truth, which was a characteristic of the "modernist" mind. Postmodernism allows for a differing ultimate reality or truth for differing individuals or groups. i.e., "What's true for you may not be true for me." The only "truth" in postmodernism is that nothing is true for everybody all the time.

The 19th century vision of those like Oliver Wendell Holmes, Jr. and Christopher Columbus Langdell at Harvard Law School has become a 21st century reality—American law no longer recognizes a Supreme and Sovereign Creator with the authority to demand obedience from His created subjects. Now judges themselves can decide what is best for society and evolve the law in any direction that furthers their own elitist concepts of societal rights and responsibilities. Today, as a result of this shift in worldview and jurisprudence, Americans have evolving rights, based not on the absolutes of the Bible, not on the Declaration of Independence, not on the Creator God, but on the State and, primarily, on the whim of judges. For all practical purposes, a postmodern judiciary, not the Creator God of the Bible, now determines what rights Americans possess. The Supreme Court has essentially usurped the authority of the Supreme Creator.

Chapter 2

Government Was God's Idea

Government is an institution ordained and created by
God for all eternity.

I. GOVERNMENT WAS ORDAINED BY GOD AS HIS DIVINE ORDER.

The concept of government is introduced in the very beginning of God's Word in the book of Genesis when God told Noah and his sons that a government of law would be established to protect the lives of men.

> *And surely your blood of your lives will I require; at the hand of every beast will I require it, and at the hand of man; at the hand of every man's brother will I require the life of man. Whoso sheddeth man's blood, by man shall his blood be shed: for in the image of God made he man.*
> —*Genesis 9:5-6*

Scripture makes it clear that God has ordained all government.

> *For there is no power but of God: the powers that be are ordained of God.*
> —*Romans 13:1b*

> *For by him were all things created, that are in heaven, and that are in earth, visible and invisible, whether they be thrones, or dominions, or principalities, or powers: all things were created by him, and for him.*
> —*Colossians 1:16*

Government is not something Man invented, nor is there only one way for Mankind to be governed. The Bible says nothing specifically about government being created "of the people, by the people, and for the people." Yet, God divinely established government as one of three divinely-created institutions:

- The Home
- The Church
- The Government

Just as with the church and the home, when we speak about the government, we are speaking about an institution divinely ordained by God and recorded in God's Book, the Bible.

II. GOVERNMENTS ARE RAISED UP BY GOD.

Whether good or bad, there has never been, and never will be, any government that God does not raise up. God has total control in the affairs of all the governments of this earth. *"By me kings reign, and princes decree justice. By me princes rule, and nobles, even all the judges of the earth."* (Proverbs 8:15-16)

Many examples exist in both the Old and New Testaments where God put into power rulers who loved and obeyed Him. (Psalm 2:6-7; Jeremiah 30:9; and Acts 13:21-22) We should always pray that only good men and women will be placed in positions of power in our nation so that all Americans can be blessed with God's promise that *"[w]hen the righteous are in authority, the people rejoice: but when the wicked beareth rule, the people mourn."* (Proverbs 29:2)

The Bible, however, contains just as many examples of God raising up wicked and unjust governments and using them to accomplish His eternal purposes. God can turn the most wicked and vile ruler's heart however He wills it. *"The king's heart is in the hand of the LORD, as the rivers of water: he turneth it whithersoever he will."* (Proverbs 21:1)

Sometimes God uses hostile powers to punish His people. (Jeremiah 51:11a) Other times He uses them to rescue His people. (Daniel 2:37, 38) At still other times, God uses wicked people to proclaim His salvation (John 19:10, 11) or to glorify His name. (Romans 9:17; Exodus 9:16) No ruler rises up in any nation unless and until God grants the power and authority to do so. Thus, when Americans stand before a court or a state legislature, or any governmental body, they are standing before an institution raised up by God, whether that arm of government is good or evil. Fortunately, in America, God has instituted a government in which all citizens, including Christians, can play an important and active role in ensuring good government.

III. GOVERNMENT IS SUSTAINED AND REMOVED AT GOD'S PLEASURE.

Governments succeed and fail according to God's good pleasure. When God ceases to sustain a government, that government is finished governing. Many Old Testament passages show how it pleased God to remove certain rulers from power.

The Book of Daniel describes how God removed Nebuchadnezzar, the King of Babylon, from power. Nebuchadnezzar was a vile man, vaunted in his imagination and almost unsurpassed in his wickedness. After he dreamed a troubling dream, he called Daniel to interpret it. Daniel reluctantly told Nebuchadnezzar that, although God had raised him to great power and authority, He was going to remove him from his position as king. For seven years, Nebuchadnezzar would go insane and live like an animal and then would be restored to the throne when he recognized that God, not the king, was in control.

This matter is by the decree of the watchers, and the demand by the word of the holy ones: to the intent that the living may know that the most High ruleth in the kingdom of men, and giveth it to whomsoever he will, and setteth up over it the basest of men.
—Daniel 4:17

The dream was fulfilled according to God's Word. Indeed, the king's sanity was restored to him when he blessed and praised God for His everlasting dominion and kingdom. Nebuchadnezzar finally declared,

And all the inhabitants of the earth are reputed as nothing: and he doeth according to his will in the army of heaven, and among the inhabitants of the earth: and none can stay his hand, or say unto him, What doest thou?
—Daniel 4:35

IV. THOSE WHO WANT TO OBEY GOD MUST OBEY GOVERNMENT.

Obedience to government is obedience to God. Conversely, to disobey government is to disobey God, which is a sin. We are to obey government because God commands it, not merely because we are politically conservative or liberal or patriotic or good citizens. In fact, Scripture tells us that we are not to be obedient to government because we are good citizens; but instead, we are good citizens when we are obedient to God.

God does not tell us to obey only a just government because there will never be a truly just government until Jesus rules and reigns in eternity. That is the beauty of our Constitution's separation of powers. Each power is required to keep other powers in check.

We Americans, and especially American Christians, should obey every part of the law that we possibly can without actually violating our faith. And that determination must be taken very seriously. Our credibility is destroyed when an opponent can demonstrate that our disobedience is not really based on our faith. Disobedience of any law for reasons unrelated to faith and conscience is disobedience to God Himself and should be considered only with much prayer and after unsuccessfully seeking every other remedy.

Fortunately, as Americans, we can still thank God for His blessing in raising up a good form of government for our nation. Our government is good primarily because our Founders based our foundational documents and laws on the laws of God.

Chapter 3

The Declaration of Independence

The Declaration of Independence, America's
founding document, was based on God's laws.

In order to be effective citizens and to honor the government that God
has graciously set over our nation, we must understand the basis for our
Constitution and for those documents that preceded it in America's history.
The Declaration of Independence is the "why" of American government,
while the Constitution is the "how." If looked at from the point of view
of a business corporation, the Declaration of Independence can be called
America's Articles of Incorporation, while the Constitution can be seen as
America's Bylaws. Just as with any business, the Bylaws may never legally
contradict the Articles of Incorporation.

I. THE DECLARATION OF INDEPENDENCE ESTABLISHES THE BIBLICAL FOUNDATIONS FOR THE CONSTITUTION.

Many critics of the Judeo-Christian influence on American law note that
the Constitution does not mention either God or the Bible. The truth is that
was not necessary because the Declaration of Independence had already
declared twelve years earlier that its basic principles of freedom and justice
come from the Creator God of the Bible. The Constitution merely added
to that foundational document the rules by which these founding biblical
principles would be put into practice. In 1897, the United States Supreme
Court said:

> *The first official action of this nation declared the foundation
> of government in these words: "We hold these truths to be self-
> evident, that all men are created equal, that they are endowed by
> their Creator with certain unalienable rights that among these are
> life, liberty, and the pursuit of happiness." While such declaration
> of principles may not have the force of organic law, or be made
> the basis of judicial decision as to the limits of right and duty,
> and while in all cases reference must be had to the organic law
> of the nation for such limits, yet the latter is but the body and the*

letter of which the former is the thought and the spirit, and it is
always safe to read the letter of the constitution in the spirit of the
Declaration of Independence.

Gulf, C. & S. F. Ry. Co. v. Ellis, 165 U.S. 150, 159 (1897).

II. THE LAWS OF NATURE AND OF NATURE'S GOD ARE THE BASIS FOR THE DECLARATION OF INDEPENDENCE.

In 21st century America, the phrase "the laws of nature and of nature's God," contained in the Declaration of Independence, is difficult to understand. As understood by our Founders, however, the "laws of nature" refer to God's unchanging principles established at Creation, while the "laws of nature's God" refer to the written Word found in the Bible. In declaring their independence from Great Britain, our Founders declared their dependence upon Providence (a favorite word used by the Founders to refer to the God of the Bible). The authors of the Declaration stated:

> *WHEN in the Course of human Events, it becomes necessary for*
> *one People to dissolve the Political Bands which have connected*
> *them with another, and to assume among the Powers of the Earth,*
> *the separate and equal Station to which the Laws of Nature and*
> *of Nature's God entitle them, a decent Respect to the Opinions of*
> *Mankind requires that they should declare the causes which impel*
> *them to the Separation.*

We think of "nature" as something physical—as mountains or trees or animals. We also think of "nature" as describing the qualities of a person or thing. However, in the 18th century, when the Declaration of Independence was written, this phrase, "the laws of nature," was understood to mean God's law, obtained through reason and science, and "the laws of nature's God" to refer to His law revealed to Mankind in the Scriptures of the Old and New Testaments. America's Founding Fathers believed that God, as the Author and Judge of natural law, formed the basis in Creation for our intuitions of right and wrong. They also believed that God is the primary context for our ability to reason and to govern ourselves. William Blackstone, the most popular expositor of law and government in America at the time the Declaration of Independence was written in 1776, expressed it this way:

> *Man, considered as a creature, must necessarily be subject to the*
> *laws of his Creator, for he is entirely a dependent being . . . as man*
> *depends absolutely upon his Maker for every thing, it is necessary*

that he should in all points conform to his Maker's will. This will of his maker is called the law of nature . . . when [God] created man, and endued him with freewill to conduct himself in all parts of life, He laid down certain immutable laws of human nature, whereby that freewill is in some degree regulated and restrained, and gave him also the faculty of reason to discover the purport of those laws. . . .

This law of nature, being coeval[2] with mankind and dictated by God himself, is of course superior in obligation to any other. It is binding over all the globe in all countries, and at all times; no human laws are of any validity, if contrary to this: and such of them as are valid derive all their force, and all their authority, mediately[3] or immediately, from this original. . . .

Upon these two foundations, the law of nature and the law of revelation, depend all human laws; that is to say, no human laws should be suffered to contradict these.[1]

Thus, the "laws of nature" are God's unwritten laws implanted in Mankind at the time of Creation. They are God's general revelation in nature (see Romans 1:18-20). The "laws of nature's God" are His written laws revealed for us in Scripture.

III. THE SELF-EVIDENT TRUTHS ESPOUSED IN THE DECLARATION OF INDEPENDENCE ARE TRUTHS THAT ARE KNOWN INTUITIVELY BY ALL MANKIND AND THEY ARE DIRECTLY REVEALED IN SCRIPTURE.

The heavens declare the glory of God; and the firmament sheweth his handiwork.
–Psalm 19:1

The heavens declare his righteousness, and all the people see his glory.
–Psalm 97:6

In the Preamble to the Declaration of Independence, Thomas Jefferson

---

[2] Defined, "Equal in age or duration; having the same age, duration or date of origin." Retrieved from http://dictionary.reference.com/browse/coeval?s=t
[3] Defined, "to settle (disputes, strikes, etc.) as an intermediary between parties; reconcile." Retrieved from: http://dictionary.reference.com/browse/mediately?s=t

spoke of "self-evident truths:"

> WE hold these Truths to be self-evident, that all Men are created equal, that they are endowed by their Creator with certain unalienable Rights, that among these are Life, Liberty and the Pursuit of Happiness. That to secure these Rights, Governments are instituted among Men, deriving their just Powers from the Consent of the Governed . . .

In the Declaration's Preamble, Jefferson based America's government on those Truths that are known intuitively by all Mankind, and that are revealed by God in the Bible—without the need for proof, discussion, or debate. For America's Founders, no discussion was needed to show that Mankind (including both male and female) is created in the image of God, just as black is not white, round is not square, and water is wet. These are all facts of nature that cannot be proven; nevertheless, as human beings we are able to reason and see the truth of them.

IV. ONE IMPORTANT SELF-EVIDENT TRUTH IN THE DECLARATION OF INDEPENDENCE IS THAT ALL MEN ARE CREATED EQUAL.

Thomas Jefferson declared that one important self-evident truth for American government is that "all Men are created equal." That truth, the equality of all men and women, relates to all humanity's equality in the sight of God. Before God all Mankind has the same nature: we are all human; we are all sinful; we are all created in His image, and we are all equally loved by Him.

That word "equal," as used in the Declaration of Independence, was not intended to mean that we will all achieve the same station in life or that we are all exactly the same in appearance, ability, assets, character, personality, or status. Instead, it is our equality before God and, therefore, our equality with respect to each other that preserves our unique creation as God's individual children, all with equal worth.

V. MANKIND'S EQUALITY IS DEMONSTRATED IN OUR UNALIENABLE RIGHTS, WHICH ARE DERIVED FROM OUR RELATIONSHIP AND DUTIES TO THE CREATOR GOD.

All Men (which includes both men and women) are equal in the sense that God has created us all, male and female, with the same unalienable rights. Because we are all created in God's image, we have a duty to respect and honor the image of God in ourselves and in others and, therefore, to honor the rights equally given by God to everyone. When others try to dishonor the image of God in us or in others, we have a corresponding duty to resist those efforts and to defend those God-given rights through our government. The unalienable rights granted to Americans in the Declaration of Independence are rights based upon the corresponding duties that we all owe to our Creator God. Our rights are intended to enable us to perform our duties to God.

Our God-given unalienable rights are sometimes called natural rights— those rights possessed by all Mankind under the laws of nature in God's creation. As part of our birthright, these natural rights cannot be sold, given away, or taken from us. In fact, we cannot rightfully give them away even if we want to. Thus, we understand that God, not government, is the source of our rights. Government is responsible to identify and protect our natural rights, but government has no power to grant or deny them.

In declaring the endowment of our unalienable rights, Thomas Jefferson was clearly influenced by George Mason's Virginia Declaration of Rights, also drafted in 1776, which said:

> *Section 1: That all men are by nature equally free and independent and have certain inherent rights, of which, when they enter into a state of society, they cannot, by any compact, deprive or divest their posterity; namely, the enjoyment of life and liberty, with the means of acquiring and possessing property, and pursuing and obtaining happiness and safety.*

VI. THE FIRST UNALIENABLE RIGHT IDENTIFIED IN THE DECLARATION OF INDEPENDENCE IS THE RIGHT TO LIFE.

The unalienable right to life is a gift from God that cannot rightfully be either surrendered or taken away. Our Declaration of Independence requires the government to protect this God-given right to life. Government may not take this right away from us or from our posterity. When a right is unalienable, even the person who holds that right is not permitted to give it away. Therefore, our government must be accountable for protecting the unalienable right to life for all people regardless of their location, their quality of life, or their burden on other individuals or on society. As William Blackstone said:

A man's limbs . . . are also the gift of the wise creator. . . . To these therefore he has a natural inherent right; and they cannot be wantonly destroyed or disabled without a manifest breach of civil liberty.[2]

This first unalienable right is the basis for America's duty to respect and defend life created by God from conception through natural death. Our government has no legitimate authority to trample upon the unalienable right to life of the pre-born, of individuals with disabilities, of the elderly, or of any other innocent person. All are equally precious in God's sight and equally created in His image. Therefore, the Declaration of Independence holds government accountable for securing the right to life for all people— no matter what their quality of life or station in society. Government only acts lawfully when it equally protects the right to life of everyone under its authority.

VII. THE UNALIENABLE RIGHT TO LIBERTY IN THE DECLARATION IS NOT A RIGHT TO ENGAGE IN LICENTIOUS BEHAVIOR.

William Blackstone described man's unalienable right to liberty as one of God's gifts to Mankind at Creation. He described this liberty as consisting *"properly in a power of acting as one thinks fit, without any restraint or control, unless by the law of nature."*[3] Algernon Sidney, another early expositor of government, saw liberty as *"the gift of God and nature"* and *"an exemption from all human laws, to which they have not given their assent."*[4]

John Locke, a Christian enlightenment thinker, expressed it this way:

> *[T]hough this be a state of liberty, yet it is not a state of license....[T]hat being all equal and independent, no one ought to harm another in his life, health, liberty or possessions; for men being all the workmanship of one omnipotent and infinitely wise Maker; all the servants of one sovereign Master, sent into the world by His order and about His business; they are His property, whose workmanship they are made to last during His, not one another's pleasure.*[5]

William Blackstone taught that Man's natural liberty has only two restraints. The first is Man's duty to obey God and His laws. The second is the restraint of a voluntary community, by which Men freely choose to form and to live under a government. Man, in forming a voluntary governmental community, thus *"obliges himself to conform to those laws, which the community has thought proper to establish."*[6] Blackstone identifies this community law, which may not contradict God's law, as *"municipal law,"* defined as a *"rule of civil conduct prescribed by the supreme power in a state commanding what is right and prohibiting what is wrong."*[7] Since, however, the laws of nature and of nature's God need no help from community, or municipal, laws in order to be established, Blackstone also points out:

> *Those rights, then, which God and nature have established, and are therefore called natural rights, such as are life and liberty, need not the aid of human laws to be more effectually invested in every man than they are; neither do they receive any additional strength when declared by the municipal laws to be inviolable[4]. On the contrary, no human legislature has power to abridge or destroy them, unless the owner shall himself commit some act that amounts to a forfeiture.*[8]

Blackstone also taught that the law of nature and of nature's God must dictate municipal laws whenever they prescribe the matter; however, where the laws of nature and of nature's God are indifferent to the matter—that is, where they do not speak to a particular issue—municipal laws may also then be enacted for the peace of society.[9] One modern example of the sort of municipal law that is "indifferent" with regard to the laws of nature and of God's law would be the government setting a particular speed limit in order to conform to community needs or preferences.

VIII. THE UNALIENABLE RIGHT TO THE PURSUIT OF HAPPINESS IS DERIVED FROM MANKIND'S DUTY TO LIVE ACCORDING TO THE MORAL LAWS OF GOD.

The unalienable right to the pursuit of happiness does not mean the right to happiness itself or to licentiousness, but, rather, as George Mason believed, it is a right to the means to reach this happy condition. As Algernon Sidney noted: *"[L]iberty . . . is not a licentiousness of doing what is pleasing to every one against the command of God."*[10]

In recognizing this right, William Blackstone also observed that individual happiness can only be attained by observing the laws of eternal justice and the unchanging moral laws of God. *"[F]or He [God] has so intimately connected, so inseparably interwoven the laws of eternal justice with the*

---

[4] Or, *"incapable of being violated"*

31

happiness of each individual, that the latter cannot be attained but by observing the former."[11] Aristotle had earlier observed, even in the days before Christ lived on earth, that good character is the indispensable condition and chief determinant of happiness.[12]

This understanding provided the basis for President George Washington's Farewell Address when he left office as America's first president in 1796 and issued a warning to the new nation regarding its attention to religion. President Washington said:

> *Of all the dispositions and habits which lead to political prosperity, Religion and morality are indispensable supports. In vain would that man claim the tribute of Patriotism, who should labor to subvert these great Pillars of human happiness, these firmest props of the duties of Men and citizens.*

IX. GOVERNMENT'S CHIEF PURPOSE IS TO SECURE MAN'S UNALIENABLE RIGHTS AS THEY HAVE BEEN BESTOWED BY GOD.

In America, our rights come from God, not from the government. Therefore, the government cannot rightfully take them away. What Uncle Sam gives, Uncle Sam can take away. But our nation's birth certificate, the Declaration of Independence, makes clear that our rights are unalienable because they come from God.

America's Founders and the authors of the Declaration of Independence believed that the purpose of government is to secure the unalienable God-given rights of Man. Conversely, the power of government is limited to protecting Man's unalienable rights to life, liberty and the pursuit of happiness. To go beyond this mandate from God would mean that government was acting outside the boundaries of its just powers.

When Thomas Jefferson said in the Declaration of Independence, *"Governments are instituted among Men,"* he proclaimed that all Men are free to live independently under the laws of nature or to choose to live in a civil society. By choosing to live in a civil society, Men authorize their community to make laws for them. As a result, governments derive *"their just Powers from the Consent of the Governed."* Because the people receive their liberty from God alone, they must freely and voluntarily agree to join together to live in a community under the authority of a government. Algernon Sidney said:

[M]en could not resign their liberty, unless they naturally had it in themselves. Resignation is a public declaration of their assent to be governed by the person to whom they resign; that is, they do by act constitute him to be their governor.[13]

The central idea of the Declaration of Independence—that the authority of government comes from the people—was the ultimate implementation of a revolutionary idea that had been developing in America in a practical way over the previous 140 years as local Bible-based commonwealths were established all along America's Eastern seaboard. As John Winthrop, the first Governor of Massachusetts, said: *"No common weale*[5] *can be founded but by free consent."*[14] The Declaration of Independence was revolutionary for people who had been governed by kings and queens for thousands of years in Europe. In 1776, Thomas Jefferson adopted for Americans an idea that had been stirring in the hearts of enlightened Christian thinkers for hundreds of years, both on the European Continent and in America. Jefferson declared that King George III's authority to govern came from God through the people, and that governing the colonies was not the King's birthright. Once the American people understood their equality, even with the King of England, they were empowered through the Declaration of Independence to withdraw their consent to his government and to freely institute their own government independent of his autocratic rule.

X. IN DECLARING THEIR INDEPENDENCE FROM GREAT BRITAIN, AMERICANS UNDERSTOOD THAT THEY WERE MAKING THEMSELVES ENTIRELY DEPENDENT UPON THE PROVIDENTIAL CARE OF A SOVEREIGN CREATOR GOD.

Thomas Jefferson's climactic closing paragraph in the Declaration of Independence reflects the general religious sentiments of his day. He appealed *"to the Supreme Judge of the World,"* thereby recognizing that most people of his day believed in the Judeo-Christian God and placed themselves under that God's authority. He reinforced this view by closing the Declaration with these words:

---

[5] Or, *"commonwealth"*

And for the support of this Declaration, with a firm Reliance on the Protection of divine Providence, we mutually pledge to each other our Lives, our Fortunes, and our sacred Honor.

In 1776, the American people understood the term "divine Providence" to mean God's providential care for Mankind and His control of the world. It was only their faith in God and their confidence that independence was His cause that gave the colonists, a ragtag bunch of patriots, the courage to pledge their lives, their fortunes and their sacred honor in declaring themselves to be free and independent of the greatest military power on earth at that time.

XI. THE FIRST AND SECOND CONTINENTAL CONGRESSES ENDED WITH THE PUBLICATION OF THE DECLARATION OF INDEPENDENCE.

Samuel Adams of Massachusetts, the founder of the colonial Committees of Correspondence, the leader of the Boston Tea Party, and the last great Massachusetts Puritan, was the first person to call for the colonists to meet and discuss what to do about the oppression of the British king. The First Continental Congress assembled in Philadelphia in September 1774 to consider some options.

The colonies had become united through the First Great Awakening, a spiritual renewal sparked only a few years before by the revivalist preaching of George Whitefield and the conversion to Christ of a large percentage of colonial Americans.[15] Their recently renewed faith united them in a way that would not have been possible earlier. King George III never imagined that the 13 independent American colonies would stick so closely together to oppose his unjust measures against them.

The First Continental Congress adjourned in October 1774 with plans to meet again the following spring. By the time the Second Continental Congress convened in May 1775, the colonists had tried every way they could think of to avoid war, but the British king was making peace impossible. With the battles of Lexington and Concord just a month earlier fresh on their minds, the colonial delegates returned to Philadelphia. On July 4, 1776, the Second Continental Congress adopted the Declaration of Independence declaring themselves independent colonies and no longer under the rule of England.

It has long been recognized that America is the only country in the history of the world that was deliberately founded on the Judeo-Christian principles of the Bible. During these early years of American history, the Bible was the source most often quoted in political writings of the day.[16]

Around the time of the two hundredth birthday of America's Constitution, Time magazine published an article called, "Looking to Its Roots," in which it recognized America's biblical origins. The article said:

> *Ours is the only country deliberately founded on a good idea. That good idea combines a commitment to man's inalienable rights with the Calvinist belief in an ultimate moral right and sinful man's obligation to do good. These articles of faith, embodied in the Declaration of Independence and in the Constitution, literally govern our lives today.* [17]

A few years earlier, in 1982, Newsweek magazine had also featured a cover story discussing the Bible's impact on America's founding. That article included these remarkable words:

> *[F]or centuries [the Bible] has exerted an unrivaled influence on American culture, politics and social life. Now historians are discovering that the Bible, perhaps even more than the Constitution, is our founding document: the source of the powerful myth of the United States as a special, sacred nation, a people called by God to establish a model society, a beacon to the world.*[18]

And just how had these revolutionary biblical ideas been promulgated among the ordinary citizens of the 13 colonies prior to 1776? These biblical principles of government had been taught to the people by the patriotic Black Regiment, the name assigned to America's colonial preachers because of the color of their robes.[19] While most of these men never donned a military uniform during the Revolutionary War, their black pulpit robes identified them as being just as important to the success of the Revolution as those who wore military uniforms.

Christianity indeed played a significant role in the development of our nation's birth certificate, the Declaration of Independence. An early American historian, Paul Johnson, wrote of this document:

There is no question that the Declaration of Independence was, to those who signed it, a religious as well as a secular act, and that the Revolutionary War had the approbation of divine providence. They had won it with God's blessing and, afterwards, they drew up their framework of government with God's blessing, just as in the 17th century the colonists had drawn up their Compacts and Charters and Orders and Instruments, with God peering over their shoulders.[20]

Chapter 4

The Articles of Confederation

The Constitution was not the first statement of bylaws
enacted by the newly free and united colonies.

In May of 1776, the delegates to the Continental Congress assembled in Philadelphia determined to make provision for how a new government "of the people" would deal with the day-to-day problems of the national entity being created by the Declaration of Independence. After a month of long consideration, on June 11, 1776, the delegates adopted a resolution to appoint a committee to determine the governmental form their new confederation of colonies should take. One member from each colony was appointed to the committee.

The new governing document proposed by this committee on November 15, 1777, was called the Articles of Confederation. This document was put into printed form and sent to the legislatures of the 13 colonies for their approval and ratification. The Articles were duly ratified by these colonial legislatures on March 2, 1781, almost five years after independence was declared from Britain, but still two years before the colonies finally won their Revolutionary War against England in 1783.

I. PROVISIONS OF THE ARTICLES OF CONFEDERATION.

The Articles of Confederation, under which the United States of America first operated, had no power of taxation, no power to regulate commerce, and no method of enforcing any measure passed by the national Congress with respect to all of the colonies. While there was a Congress composed of delegates from every colony in the union, there was no provision for an executive officer. The closest thing to a president was the presiding officer of Congress elected by his peers for one year. Congress itself was a single chamber body.

Under the Articles of Confederation, each state retained its independent sovereignty, and only those powers granted specifically to the United States could be exercised by the national Congress. Those powers primarily included mutual defense against common enemies and a general bond of mutual friendship and assistance with regard to the general welfare of all the states.

The Articles provided for mutual privileges and immunities for free citizens, free ingress and egress among the various states, free trade and commerce among the states, extradition of felons, full faith and credit to the acts of every other state, a means of resolution of property disputes between the states, regulation of common currency, weights and measures, a common administration of Indian affairs, and a common postal service. The Congress appointed its own presiding officer, formed such committees as it deemed necessary, and raised needed military forces from the states, which individually bore the cost of equipping them.

II. THE ARTICLES OF CONFEDERATION ACKNOWLEDGED GOD.

Like virtually every early American document, the Articles of Confederation acknowledged God, referring to Him as "*the Great Governor of the World.*" The document ended with these words by which each signatory ratifying the Articles recognized the hand of God in raising up their new government:

> *And Whereas it hath pleased the Great Governor of the World to incline the hearts of the legislatures we respectively represent in Congress, to approve of, and to authorize us to ratify the said Articles of Confederation and perpetual Union.*

III. THE ARTICLES OF CONFEDERATION BECAME INSUFFICIENT TO MEET THE NEEDS OF THE NEW UNITED STATES OF AMERICA.

While the Articles of Confederation saw the new union of states through the perils of the Revolutionary War, which ended in 1783, that document's basic structural flaws made it more and more unworkable over time. One such flaw was that every legislative measure had to be approved by all of the individual states; and getting all the states to agree unanimously on anything was very difficult.

In August of 1786, three years after the successful conclusion of the War for Independence, a committee of the Congress met at Annapolis, Maryland and issued a report recommending alterations to the Articles in the interests of the Union. Rhode Island announced that it wanted nothing to do with any revision of the Articles and would refuse to approve any alterations. In fact, no delegates from Rhode Island attended the Constitutional Convention when it finally convened.

The committee that met at Annapolis in August of 1786 also issued a call for a meeting of the colonies to discuss the proposed changes the committee was recommending. That meeting convened on May 25, 1787 in Philadelphia. George Washington was unanimously elected to preside over what was to become the Constitutional Convention.

Chapter 5

The Constitutional Convention of 1787

Drafting the new Constitution required the
miraculous intervention of God.

The Convention that was called by the states in 1787 did not meet initially to draft a new Constitution. The stated purpose of this meeting was merely to revise the Articles of Confederation. The federal Congress had earlier adopted a resolution that suggested all the colonies should meet together to consider the needs of the Union and report their recommendations to Congress. Every state was invited to send delegates to this meeting.

The vast majority of the fifty-five state delegates who attended the meeting in Philadelphia, later known as the Constitutional Convention, were professing Christians. Only Benjamin Franklin and James Wilson of Pennsylvania were known to be Deists (those who believed in God, but did not believe in God's revelation or authority; and who believed that God had created the world and its natural laws, but took no further part in its functioning). It is also thought that Hugh Williamson of North Carolina and James McClurg of Virginia may have been non-Trinitarian. Historian John Eidsmoe concludes that, at most, 5.5% of those attending the Constitutional Convention were Deists. Most of the Convention delegates had been educated in schools such as Princeton where theology and a serious study of the Bible were required subjects. Everyone who attended these schools, whatever their intended profession, received the same basic Christian theological training as seminarians.[1]

I. THE CONVENTION OF 1787 SOON BECAME THE CONSTITUTIONAL CONVENTION.

As discussed, when the colonial representatives first met in 1787 for what we now call the Constitutional Convention, they were not meeting for the purpose of drafting a brand new constitution. However, the Articles of Confederation, which had been written in 1777 and ratified in 1781, no longer seemed adequate for the needs of the newly united states.

Alexander Hamilton said of the nation as it was being governed under the Articles of Confederation: "*In America . . . the government of the Union has gradually dwindled into a state of decay, approaching nearly to annihilation.*"[2] Soon after the delegates began their attempt to revise the Articles of Confederation, Edmond Jennings Randolph, representing Virginia, stood up and proposed a complete overhaul of the Articles although, ironically, by the end of the Convention, he along with George Mason of Virginia and two of the delegates from Massachusetts were the only delegates who chose not to sign the document.

To make a more workable government, the Constitutional Convention first decided to adopt the provision that it would take only nine of the 13 states, essentially a two-thirds majority, for proposals to be enacted. This would be the same majority required for ratification of the new document itself. Nevertheless, even with only nine states required for agreement, the changes did not come easily.

II. THE DELEGATES AGREED THAT THE FINAL DRAFTING OF THE NEW CONSTITUTION WAS A MIRACLE OF GOD.

Modern Americans tend to glamorize the writing of the Constitution; however, the process was anything but glamorous. The Convention met at Independence Hall in Philadelphia between May and September of 1787. The weather was hot and muggy. The pace was slow going. Tempers flared. The delegates seemed to ramble in circles for weeks on end. Some delegates left—prematurely and permanently.

There was a great deal of acrimony in the early days of the Convention, especially between the more populated states and the less populated states as they discussed how they should be represented in the new united government. There were also bitter conflicts over slavery as some, particularly in the North, loathed the practice, while others, particularly in the South, depended upon it for their economic viability.

In light of all the difficulties encountered in writing the Constitution, Alexander Hamilton reflected back years later about the Constitutional government that emerged from this Convention:

> *For my own part, I sincerely esteem it a system which, without the finger of God, never could have been suggested and agreed upon by such a diversity of interests.*[3]

The Convention proceedings were so difficult that at one point, when Alexander Hamilton had left temporarily, George Washington wrote him a letter disheartened about the whole enterprise:

> *I almost despair of seeing a favourable issue to the proceedings of the Convention, and do therefore repent [of] having had any agency in the business.*[4]

The Convention was deteriorating so badly that even Washington, its president, was beginning to regret being there! But when the delegates had finally agreed on a workable Constitution and the Convention adjourned, Washington described the outcome as miraculous:

> *It appears to me, then, little short of a miracle, that the Delegates from so many different States (which States you know are also different from each other in their manners, circumstances, and prejudices), should unite in forming a system of national Government, so little liable to well founded objections.*[5]

James Madison also believed that a supernatural work of God had taken place at Independence Hall. He said:

> *The real wonder is that so many difficulties should have been surmounted, and surmounted with a unanimity almost as unprecedented as it must have been unexpected. It is impossible for any man of candor to reflect on this circumstance without partaking of the astonishment. It is impossible for the man of pious reflection not to perceive in it a finger of that Almighty hand which has been so frequently and signally extended to our relief in the critical stages of the revolution.*[6]

James Madison often spoke of what some have called the "miracle in Philadelphia."[7] His words are memorialized on the wall of the Madison Building in the Library of Congress in Washington, D.C.:

> *THE HAPPY UNION OF THESE STATES IS A WONDER; THEIR CONSTITUTION A MIRACLE; THEIR EXAMPLE THE HOPE OF LIBERTY THROUGHOUT THE WORLD.*

Historian and author Catherine Drinker Bowen described the atmosphere at the convention on June 9, 1787. The proceedings, which had begun in May, seemed to be going nowhere. *"At this point,"* she writes, *"and indeed throughout the month of June, one marvels the Convention did not dissolve* and the members go home. *The large states were if possible more stubborn than the small."* [8]

Progress was often slow going and discouraging. But men like George Mason were persistent. Mason, who ironically did not sign the final document, declared that he would *"bury his bones in Philadelphia rather than quit with no solution found."* [9]

By June 27, 1787, things had not improved. A Georgia delegate, William Few, described the morning of June 28 as *"an awful and critical moment. If the Convention had then adjourned, the dissolution of the union of the states seemed inevitable."* [10]

But then the miracle happened! On that day, June 28, 1787, a breakthrough occurred. After weeks and weeks of frustratingly little progress, a wonderfully moving speech, made on the Convention floor, caused the tide to turn. Benjamin Franklin, who gave that speech, was a Deist. He was not one of the vast majority of Christian delegates to the Convention who believed strongly in the Judeo-Christian God of the Bible. Nevertheless, Dr. Franklin made an impassioned speech, reminding his fellow delegates that God had always answered their prayers as a nation, even when they were at war. Now that things were going so badly, should they not again turn to the Lord for help? Besides, asked Franklin, how could they expect to successfully create a new nation without God's help?

Dr. Benjamin Franklin's words were recorded for posterity on that miraculous day:

Mr. President:

The small progress we have made after 4 or five weeks close attendance & continual reasonings with each other – our different sentiments on almost every question, several of the last producing as many noes as ays, is methinks a melancholy proof of the imperfection of the Human Understanding. We indeed seem to feel our own want of political wisdom, since we have been running about in search of it.

In this situation of this Assembly, groping as it were in the dark to find political truth, and scarce able to distinguish it when presented to us, how has it happened, Sir, that we have not hitherto once thought of humbly applying to the Father of lights to illuminate our understandings? In the beginning of the Contest with G. Britain, when we were sensible of danger we had daily prayer in this room for the divine protection – Our prayers, Sir, were heard, & they were graciously answered. All of us who were engaged in the struggle must have observed frequent instances of a superintending providence in our favor. To that kind providence we owe this happy opportunity of consulting in peace on the means of establishing our future national felicity. And have we now forgotten that powerful friend? or do we imagine we no longer need his assistance? I have lived, Sir, a long time, and the longer I live, the more convincing proofs I see of this truth – that God Governs in the affairs of men. And if a sparrow cannot fall to the ground without his notice, is it probable that an empire can rise without his aid? We have been assured, Sir, in the sacred writings, that "except the Lord build the House, they labor in vain that build it." [Psalm 127:1a] I firmly believe this; and I also believe that without his concurring aid we shall succeed in this political building no better than the Builders of Babel: We shall be divided by our little partial local interests; our projects will be confounded, and we ourselves shall become a reproach and bye word down to future ages. And what is worse, mankind may hereafter from this unfortunate instance, despair of establishing Governments by Human wisdom and leave it to chance, war and conquest.

I therefore beg leave to move – that henceforth prayers imploring the assistance of Heaven, and its blessing on our deliberations, be held in this Assembly every morning before we proceed to business, and that one or more of the Clergy of this City be requested to officiate in that Service.[11]

Immediately after Dr. Franklin spoke, Roger Sherman of Connecticut seconded his motion for prayer. Many of those who saw and heard the oldest man among them make this earnest plea were deeply moved. New Jersey delegate Jonathan Dayton reported what he saw after Dr. Franklin's impassioned request for prayer:

The Doctor sat down; and never did I behold a countenance at once so dignified and delighted as was that of Washington at the close of the address; nor were the members of the convention generally less affected. The words of the venerable Franklin fell upon our ears with a weight and authority, even greater than we may suppose an oracle to have had in a Roman senate![12]

44

But there were others who had their own practical reasons for opposing the motion to begin each day with prayer. Dr. Franklin's motion for opening the sessions with prayer every morning was not acted upon because the Convention lacked funds to pay a clergyman, and also because the delegates were afraid that news of outside clergymen coming to assist in services would start rumors that dissension was breaking out in the Convention.

Edmund Jennings Randolph of Virginia proposed a compromise measure: "*That a sermon be preached at the request of the convention on the 4th of July, the anniversary of Independence; & thenceforward prayers be used in ye Convention every morning.*"[13] Benjamin Franklin himself seconded this substitute motion.

Within a week, on July 4, the entire assembly worshiped together at a nearby church in Philadelphia. While some difficulties continued to arise before the conclusion of the Convention's business in September, the delegates never returned to the fruitless acrimony that had existed prior to June 28. Dr. Franklin's call for prayer played an important role in reminding the delegates at a critical time that without God's help all their efforts would be in vain.

On September 17, 1787, the final draft of the new Constitution was agreed upon. It was signed by 39 of the 55 delegates and transmitted to Congress. From there, Congress forwarded the document to the legislatures of the 13 states for approval and ratification, although approval from only nine of the 13 states was required for the document to be put into effect. On June 21, 1788, New Hampshire became the ninth state to ratify the Constitution, followed by Virginia and New York shortly thereafter. On March 4, 1789, the first Congress of the new government was seated and began operating under the new Constitution.

This new document, the Constitution, included its seven original articles, but it did not include a Bill of Rights, something Congress had to promise would be added in order to have the document ratified by a sufficient number of states. The Bill of Rights, the first ten amendments to the Constitution, was proposed to the legislatures of the states in September, 1789. Within a few months, North Carolina and Rhode Island ratified the Constitution, becoming the last two of the original 13 colonies to do so. Interestingly, these final ratifications did not occur until after the first Congress went into session.

The new federal government went into operation in 1789, with its temporary capital in New York City. The capital was moved to Philadelphia in 1790, and, finally, to Washington, D.C., in 1800.

Chapter 6

The Constitution

The Constitution represents a compromise between those
who desired a strong central, or federal, government
and those who wanted to leave the greater power with
individual states.

America's Founding Fathers who drafted the Constitution attempted to give the federal government enough power to carry out the functions intended, while permitting the states to retain enough power to safeguard the people from a tyrannical central government. Thus, the Constitution set up a system of checks and balances so that no one branch of the federal government could have absolute control. For example, the president could veto any act passed by both houses of Congress, but Congress could override a presidential veto. Likewise, the Supreme Court could declare an act of Congress unconstitutional, but only the executive branch was empowered to enforce a decision of the Supreme Court.

I. THE BIBLICAL UNDERSTANDING OF MAN'S SINFULNESS WAS THE GUIDING PRINCIPLE BEHIND THE CHECKS AND BALANCES IN THE UNITED STATES CONSTITUTION.

Even as our Founding Fathers were agonizing and compromising over the details of the Constitution, many of them recognized that something great was taking place among them. They were pursuing a course of action that had never before been pursued in all of human history. They were creating a document that would provide the newly independent colonies with self-government and freedom. Since then, the model they crafted has been admired and copied around the world. But before America could give the gift of self-government to the world, God gave the gift of freedom and self-government to America.

The biblical understanding of the sinfulness of man was the guiding principle behind the United States Constitution. The framers of the Constitution drew their inspiration from the Bible. They intended for America to be one nation under God. They had no intention of establishing an agnostic or atheistic state.

James Madison played an especially significant role in shaping the American Constitution. While some claim it is an exaggeration, he is often called the Father of the Constitution or its chief architect. Whatever view one adopts, there is no question that Madison's influence in helping to frame the new government was invaluable. And Madison's view of government and law had been shaped primarily by his understanding of biblical Christianity.

As a Virginian, Madison would have been expected to study at the Anglican College of William and Mary. Instead, he chose to attend the College of New Jersey (now called Princeton) where he sat under the direct tutelage of Dr. John Witherspoon, a prominent Bible-believing patriot who later became the only minister to sign the Declaration of Independence. During Madison's stay at Princeton, a great revival took place, and it was believed that he was a participant in that revival. Contemporary historians report that on Madison's return to Virginia from Princeton, he began to conduct worship services in his father's house. When he announced his candidacy for the Virginia Legislature, his opponents objected, saying that he was better suited for the pulpit than for the legislature.

Perhaps the most important lesson Madison learned from his Princeton education was his firm belief in the biblical doctrine of man's inherent sinfulness. Because of man's sin, he believed that government must institute a rigorous system of checks and balances to protect its citizens from tyranny. His concept of checks and balances took into account the temptation in man's nature toward greed and selfishness. It withdrew from any one man, or from any group of men, the power to become tyrannical. In 1787, Madison wrote: "*All men having power ought to be distrusted to a certain degree.*"[1]

James Madison was not alone among the Founders in professing the Christian doctrine of original sin and insisting that this theological concept be incorporated into the new government through an elaborate system of checks and balances. The Founding Fathers all knew that because Man was sinful, total power should never be vested in any one person.

Even Benjamin Franklin, who generally claimed not to place faith in the Bible, recognized Mankind's natural propensity toward despotism when he used a biblical example to acknowledge human nature. He said: "*There is scarce a king in a hundred who would not, if he could, follow the example of Pharaoh, get first all the people's money, then all their lands, and then make them and their children servants forever."* [2]

II. A SECTION BY SECTION ANALYSIS OF THE CONSTITUTION

The Constitution consists of seven articles setting up the government of the United States of America. The text of the Constitution has, by and large, remained unchanged for more than two hundred years, although the interpretation of that text by the courts has changed dramatically over time. This section presents an overview of the key provisions and a brief commentary on each article. (See Appendix 1 for the complete text of the Constitution.)

A. The Preamble

> *We the people of the United States, in order to form a more perfect Union, establish justice, insure domestic Tranquility, provide for the common defense, promote the General Welfare, and secure the Blessings of Liberty, to ourselves and our Posterity, do ordain and establish this Constitution for the United States of America.*

The Preamble to the Constitution is not law; it is merely a declaration of the intent and purpose of the document. The Constitution's signing statement indicates that 1787, the date the Constitution was signed, was the twelfth year *"of the Independence of the United States of America."* This implies that the signers recognized that the union had already been in existence for 12 years, with the Declaration of Independence originally stating the purpose for independence. This demonstrates that the Constitution both recognizes and incorporates the foundational principles of the Declaration of Independence, which were based on a recognition of the natural and revealed laws of a Sovereign Creator God. This is one reason why people who claim the Constitution was not based on the God of the Bible are mistaken.

When the Preamble states that the Constitution is designed to *"secure the Blessings of Liberty,"* it recognizes a key principle of the Declaration of Independence—that those *"Blessings"* are bestowed by God and are merely recognized and secured by the government. As explained by one writer, *"By calling the advantages of liberty 'blessings,' the Constitution . . . nonetheless, in its understanding of the connection between happiness and virtue, aligns itself decisively with traditional moral philosophy and moral theology."* [3]

B. Article I: The Legislature

The legislature is the first branch of government discussed in the Constitution. This placement attests to the prominence assigned by the Founders to the representatives of the people elected in each state.

1. Article I: section 1: The Legislature

Congress alone, as stipulated by this section of the Constitution, possesses the exclusive responsibility and authority to determine the need for and to enact binding laws for the nation. Article I reflects the overarching revolutionary American concept that the people, through an elected legislature, are sovereign, not a monarch or an elite ruling body. Although legislation may be recommended by the executive branch of government, or even by individual citizens or groups of citizens, the responsibility for enacting legislation rests exclusively with the legislative branch. The legislative branch also has the power to set the scope and jurisdiction of the judicial branch of government, with the exceptions of those specific enumerations of power listed in Article III.

Although Congress may not grant legislative power to the executive branch of government, Congress today does, in fact, delegate a great deal of regulatory authority to certain agencies, such as Health and Human Services and the Environmental Protection Agency. Such regulatory agencies are not prohibited by the Constitution, but the Constitution does not require them. The regulations enacted by these various agencies have the force of administrative law and they must be compatible with the Constitution. However, such regulatory administrative laws are far more numerous today than was likely anticipated by the Founders—and they are far more burdensome to the people.

Today, several hundred federal agencies employ nearly 3 million people.[4] The first official census of the United States in 1790 recorded a total population of less than 4 million people.[5] That means that our current federal government alone employs almost as many people as the entire population of the United States in 1789 when the Constitution was adopted.

Congressional authority to act under the Constitution can be divided into two categories: enumerated powers and implied powers. Enumerated powers are certain particular endowments of power specifically given to Congress in Article 1, section 8 of the Constitution. "Implied powers" are those necessary in order to effectuate any of Congress's enumerated powers. The authority for these implied powers is derived from the enumerated power to *make all laws which shall be necessary and proper for carrying into Execution the foregoing [enumerated] Powers.*"

The Constitution gives explicit instructions for the organization of a bicameral legislature. Pursuant to this section, Congress is to be made up of two houses—The House of Representatives and the Senate.

2. Article I: section 2: The House of Representatives

In the House of Representatives, the number of congressional delegates is determined by each state's population. Following a national census every ten years, the number of representatives assigned to each state is reapportioned. Each state determines the shape and location of its own congressional districts.

In order for a person to qualify to take office in the House of Representatives, he or she must be at least twenty-five years old and must have been a United States citizen for at least seven years. The requirement that a House member must have been a citizen for seven years is further proof that the Constitution recognized the union had already been in existence prior to the ratification of the Constitution and, therefore, incorporated the provisions of the Declaration of Independence.

The requirements for serving in the House, particularly the age provision, have not always been followed closely. For example, the youngest person to ever serve in the House was William Charles Cole Claiborne of Tennessee, who was only twenty-two years old, and was seated by a special resolution of the House.

Another constitutional provision governing the House of Representatives includes the election, or re-election, of its members by the people every two years. The House also chooses its own Speaker and other officers, and has the sole power to impeach the President or members of the federal judiciary; however, only the Senate has the power to convict on impeachment charges and remove that person from office.

3. Article I: section 3: The Senate

The Senate is comprised of two delegates from each state, no matter how large or small. Originally, Senators were chosen by the various state legislatures, not by a vote of the general population of the state. Since 1913, with the adoption of the Seventeenth Amendment, Senators have been elected by all the citizens of each state in a popular election.

To qualify as a senatorial candidate, a person must be at least thirty years of age and a citizen of the United States for at least nine years. However, the youngest person ever to serve in the Senate was John Eaton in 1818, who was then only twenty-eight years old. In more recent times, Senator Rush Holt of West Virginia was only twenty-nine years of age when he was elected in 1935. It was determined at that time that he could not be sworn in until he reached his thirtieth birthday.

The Senate also chooses its own officers, with the exception that the vice president shall serve as the president of the Senate. The vice president has no vote in the Senate unless that body is equally divided, in which case the vice president casts the deciding vote.

The Constitution divides certain powers and procedures that are specific to only one house of Congress. This is part of an internal system of legislative checks and balances. For example, while the House of Representatives has the sole power to impeach, or to bring charges against a sitting president, federal judges, or justices of the Supreme Court, the Senate is given the "*sole Power to try all impeachments*," or to determine whether the person impeached is actually guilty of the charges. The two legislative bodies do not always agree. Only two U.S. presidents have ever been impeached— President Bill Clinton in 1998 and President Andrew Johnson in 1868. Neither man was convicted and removed from office by the Senate. President Richard Nixon resigned from the office of president rather than face impeachment in 1974.

After the House has impeached a president, the Senate sits under oath to conduct an impeachment trial with the Chief Justice of the Supreme Court designated to preside over the trial. If convicted by the Senate, punishment is limited to removal from office and disqualification to hold any future elective or appointed office in the United States. A conviction or lack thereof however, does not disqualify that person from being indicted or tried later in the proper court after leaving office, and punished as the law provides. In President Clinton's case, although he was not convicted and removed from office by the Senate, his bar license was later suspended in Arkansas, the state in which he was licensed to practice law.

4. Article I: section 4: Elections

This section requires that the Congress meet at least once during every year. While Congress may at any time enact laws to control certain aspects of elections, the Constitution grants to state legislatures the power to control the dates, times, and manner of conducting and certifying elections. The manner in which the state of Florida chose to certify its election became an issue in the presidential election of 2000, and the United States Supreme Court eventually permitted Florida's certification for President George W. Bush over then-Vice-President Al Gore.

5. Article I: section 5: Rules of Procedure

Both the House and Senate are given the right to determine their own rules of operation. They may by subpoena compel witnesses to appear and testify before them and they may hold in contempt any witnesses who do not appear or do not answer questions. Such witnesses may also be found guilty of perjury for giving false testimony under oath, with penalties including fines and imprisonment. The House and Senate also have the power to punish their own members for unseemly behavior or misconduct, and a two-thirds majority of each chamber may expel a member.

The Constitution requires Congress to keep records of its deliberations and to publish these records, with the exception of any matters requiring secrecy. This *Congressional Record* is available to any interested citizen.

6. Article I: section 6: Compensation

Members of Congress are compensated for their service, interestingly, at a rate they themselves determine. One of the privileges of office includes immunity from arrest while attending a legislative session or while traveling to or from such sessions, except for offenses of treason, felony, or breach of the peace. Except for actual charges of libel, Congress members are immune from liability while performing their duties of office. Congress members may not simultaneously serve in other government offices, including appointive offices or the military, during their term of service in the Congress.

7. Article I: section 7: Revenue Bills

While the Senate may propose or concur with amendments as with other bills, only the House of Representatives may propose bills for raising revenues (taxes). This provision does not prevent the Senate from amending revenue bills, however.

When a bill has passed in both legislative chambers, it is sent to the president who must either sign it, veto it, or do neither. If the president does not sign or veto the bill, it automatically becomes law without his signature in 10 days, excepting Sundays (another reflection of our Judeo-Christian heritage), so long as Congress is in session. If Congress is not in session when the 10 days is up, the bill dies. This is called a pocket veto. If the President physically vetoes a bill (as opposed to the pocket veto), he must return the bill to the legislature, stating his objections, whereupon the bill may be reconsidered and passed without the president's signature by a two-thirds majority of the membership present in both chambers. The date on which the president signs the bill or both chambers override the president's veto, or the day designated in the bill itself, is the date on which that bill becomes law.

8. Article I: section 8: Enumerated Powers

The enumerated powers of Congress are listed in this section of the Constitution and are discussed below. At the head of the list of powers given to the Congress is the power to uniformly *"lay and collect Taxes, Duties, Imposts and Excises, to pay the Debts and provide for the common Defense and general Welfare of the United States."* Other enumerations set forth in section 8 include the power to do the following:

- Borrow money on the credit of the U.S.;
- Regulate commerce with foreign nations, among the several states, and with the Indian Tribes;
- Establish uniform laws on naturalization and bankruptcy;
- Coin money and fix the standard of weights and measures;
- Provide for the punishment of counterfeiting the securities and current coin of the U.S.;
- Establish post offices and post roads;
- Promote the progress of science and useful arts through copyright, patents and trademarks;
- Constitute tribunals (courts) inferior to the Supreme Court;
- Define and punish piracies and felonies committed on the high seas, and offenses against the Law of Nations;
- Declare war, grant letters of marque and reprisal, and make rules concerning captures on land and water;
- Raise and support an army;
- Provide and maintain a navy;
- Make rules for the government and regulation of the land and naval forces;
- Provide for calling forth the militia to execute the laws of the Union, suppress insurrections and repel invasions;
- Provide for organizing, arming, and disciplining the militia, and for governing any part of them as may be employed in the service of the United States;
- Exercise exclusive legislation in all cases whatsoever, over the District of Columbia and all places purchased by the consent of the legislature for forts, magazines, arsenals, dock yards, and other needful buildings; and
- Make all laws necessary and proper for the carrying into execution of the enumerated powers, and all other powers vested by the Constitution in the Government of the United States.

The authorization for Congress "*to lay and collect taxes, duties, imposts and excises*" includes those duties on imported goods, excises on utilities, consumption taxes on goods and services, as well as income taxes, which were later authorized by the Sixteenth Amendment. Tax money must be used for the common defense or general welfare of the United States, provisions which have become very broadly interpreted. Courts have held that the collection of taxes is not subject to due process under the Fifth Amendment because of the need for government to collect the revenues needed to operate. The government may seize personal property and may even ignore complaints about the validity of the taxes assessed. An act of Congress for the general welfare must be effective for the entire nation and may not be specific to a particular area; however, certain local projects are determined to be good for the overall general welfare of the United States, establishing the precedent for what is often called "pork barrel" legislation, benefiting particular congressional districts.

Congress may borrow money, a power it has delegated to the Federal Reserve System, which now has complete control of currency in the United States. The Congress may also regulate international and interstate commerce, a power that has also been broadly interpreted. Courts have interpreted the commerce clause to enable Congress to regulate any activity that might have a reasonably substantial impact on interstate commerce. Courts have held relatively few areas to be outside of Congress's commerce authority.

Congress has power over uniform bankruptcy laws and over naturalization of aliens and immigrants. It has the power to coin money, a power that has also been delegated to the Federal Reserve. Congress has the power to uniformly punish counterfeiting and the power to fix the standards of weights and measurements in a uniform manner.

Congress has delegated to itself very broad powers under its regulation of the postal system. It also has power over patents and copyrights and jurisdiction to define and punish piracies and felonies on the high seas.

Another power of Congress is that of establishing federal judicial tribunals below the level of the Supreme Court, discussed in Article III of the Constitution. Congress has the power to grant or restrict the jurisdiction of lower federal courts and of the U.S. Supreme Court where jurisdiction is not specifically enumerated in Article III. However, Congress may not exercise this power in a manner that would violate the due process rights of citizens under the Fifth Amendment.

Congress has the power to declare war, to declare an end to war, and to raise and support armies and other military forces, including the National Guard. Congress may seize enemy property within the United States, while its own citizens' due process rights must be respected except for the most imminent dangers. Congress has the power to acquire and administer property within the boundaries of the various states. This includes park areas, wildlife refuge areas, and forestry preserves.

Another broad power granted to the Congress is the power to enact *"all necessary and proper"* laws for executing its enumerated powers. These are the "implied" powers of Congress and grant very broad discretion to the legislature. Congressional laws may be challenged in federal courts as being unconstitutional.

9. Article I: section 9: Prohibited Powers

The specific provision in the first clause of this section was included as a compromise in order to achieve agreement on the Constitution between the northern states that wanted to eliminate slavery and the southern states that believed slavery was essential to their economy. This clause granted the South a twenty-year reprieve in its conduct of the slave trade; however, in deference to the North, it prohibited the importation of slaves into the United States after the year 1808.

Other items covered in this section include the provision of a judicial *habeas corpus* ("to have the body") in cases where there is a question as to the legitimacy of detaining persons. A writ of *habeas corpus* requires a judicial review of circumstances surrounding a person's imprisonment or restraint. Bills of Attainder (punishment without benefit of trial) and *ex post facto* laws (punishment for an act committed before legislation made the act a crime) are prohibited since these could annul individual rights.

Other provisions prohibit titles of nobility, which would grant certain individuals favored treatment. Certain powers are denied to states, such as the power to enter into foreign treaties and to levy taxes on exports from the state.

C. Article II: The Executive Branch

The executive power under the Constitution is vested in the president, who holds office for a term of four years. Although President Franklin D. Roosevelt was elected to four terms in office, the Twenty-third Amendment now limits presidents to two terms in office. Executive powers are broad, including regulatory powers granted to the executive by the legislature and the power to issue Executive Orders, which have the force of law. The basic constitutional duties of the president, however, are to see that the acts of the Congress are properly and faithfully administered.

1. Article II, section 1: Electoral College, Qualifications, Succession, etc.

Unlike members of Congress, the president is not elected to office by the popular vote of the people, but rather by an Electoral College. In fact, several times in our nation's history the candidate receiving the greatest number of popular votes has failed to win in the Electoral College:

- In 1824, Andrew Jackson received more popular votes than John Quincy Adams.

- In 1876, Samuel J. Tilden received more popular votes than Rutherford B. Hayes.

- In 1888, Grover Cleveland received more popular votes than Benjamin Harrison.

- In 2000, Al Gore received more popular votes than George W. Bush.

Part of Article II Section 1 describes the Electoral College; however, the Twelfth Amendment later changed how the College operates. Instead of deciding the presidential election merely by a national popular vote, under the Electoral College, each state chooses a number of electors that is equal to the combined number of federal senators and representatives for that state to represent them in the Electoral College. When citizens vote for candidates for president and vice president, they are actually voting to determine which set of electors will represent their state in the Electoral College. Different states have differing methods of determining who these members of the Electoral College will be; however, these decisions are made by the individual state legislatures.

Following a presidential election, each state certifies its slate of electors, based upon which party's candidate has won its state's popular vote. The electors then meet and cast their ballots. It is presumed that electors will vote for the candidate who won the popular vote in their state and who represents their political party; however, they are not legally required to do so and electors are technically able to vote in the Electoral College for whichever candidate they prefer.

Use of the Electoral College levels the playing field for voters in large and small states and in urban and rural areas. If elections were decided based only on the national popular vote, more populous states and large cities would have greater power to elect a president. Candidates might completely avoid campaigning in less populated states and rural areas.

The candidate receiving the greatest number of votes in the Electoral College, "*if such Number be a Majority of the whole Number of Electors appointed,*" becomes president. There have been two times in our nation's history when the Electoral College has failed to reach a majority. In such cases, the election is decided by the House of Representatives.

- In 1800, Thomas Jefferson and Aaron Burr each received seventy-three electoral votes. The House chose Jefferson to be president.

- In 1824, John Quincy Adams received eighty-four electoral votes, and Andrew Jackson received ninety-nine. Even though Jackson had the most electoral votes, he did not have a majority "*of the whole Number of Electors appointed,*" so the vote went to the House, which selected Adams.

In the 2000 election, had the candidates not taken the controversy over the certification of votes in Florida to the United States Supreme Court, the election might have gone to the House of Representatives, controlled at that time by the Republicans, which would most likely have selected George W. Bush over Al Gore.

To qualify as a presidential candidate, a person must be at least thirty-five years of age, a natural born citizen, and a resident of the United States for at least fourteen years. This section also sets the succession to the office of president either through death or removal. It also sets the president's compensation, which must remain fixed during his term in office, and provides for the president's oath of office.

2. Article II, section 2: Powers

The enumerated presidential powers include the power to be Commander in Chief of the military forces; the power to grant reprieves and pardons for offenses against the United States in all cases except impeachment; the power to make treaties with the advice and consent of the Senate; and the power to nominate, and with the Senate's advice and consent, to appoint ambassadors, judges, and all other officers of the United States whose appointments are not otherwise provided for by the Constitution.

3. Article II, section 3: Recess Powers

The president's powers include the power to fill vacancies during legislative recesses (such as recess appointments of judges or executive officers). These appointments must expire no later than the end of the next session of the Senate. The president is required to provide the Congress with a State of the Union message, which for much of our nation's history was given in writing rather than orally. The president also has the power to recommend legislation, convene or adjourn the legislature in an emergency, conduct foreign diplomacy, and issue commissions for military officers.

4. Article II, section 4: Removal from Office

The president or vice president may be impeached by the House of Representatives, and removed from office upon conviction by the Senate of treason, bribery, or other high crimes and misdemeanors. These terms are not specifically defined; however, generally a high crime is considered to be a felony, while a misdemeanor is a lesser crime.

D. *Article III: The Judiciary*

The federal court system derives its power from Article III, which provides for one Supreme Court and *"such Inferior courts as the Congress may from time to time ordain and establish."* Our current federal court system consists of three levels: district courts, circuit courts, and the Supreme Court. In addition, there are several specialized courts, such as tax courts, admiralty courts, bankruptcy courts, etc. The nine Justices of the Supreme Court and the judges of inferior (lower) federal courts are appointed to office and serve for life, unless impeached.

There have not always been nine members serving on the Supreme Court. At America's founding, there were only five Supreme Court Justices. During the presidency of Franklin D. Roosevelt, he attempted to increase the number of Justices serving on the Court to 15, no doubt to gain a majority of votes to ensure the constitutionality of New Deal legislation. This action was described at the time as "packing the court," but the plan did not succeed.

As with the other two branches of government, the judicial powers are specifically enumerated. The federal judiciary has limited jurisdiction to hear cases. The specific parameters of federal jurisdiction include all cases arising from the following: the Constitution; the laws of the United States; treaties; cases involving ambassadors; cases of admiralty and maritime law; whenever the United States is a party; and controversies between two or more states or their citizens. Additional jurisdiction may be granted or withheld by the Congress. Congress is granted the constitutional authority to establish or abolish lower federal courts and to determine their jurisdiction.

All federal judges, who are appointed by the president with the consent of the Senate, serve for life unless impeached. Their compensation may not be lowered during their time in office.

Metaphorically speaking, the Constitution provides that the executive branch be given the power of the sword, while the legislative branch be given the power of the purse. The only power enumerated in the Constitution and foreseen by most for the judicial branch was the power of persuasion and of deciding specific legal cases as they arose. Because the Court was given no power to enforce its decisions, most of the Founding Fathers never envisioned the possibility of a Supreme Court that could become an elite ruling oligarchy. One important exception was Thomas Jefferson who feared the Court could eventually claim too much power:

> *"It has long been my opinion, and I have never shrunk from its expression,. . . that the germ of dissolution of our Federal Government is in the constitution of the Federal Judiciary--an irresponsible body (for impeachment is scarcely a scare-crow), working like gravity by night and by day, gaining a little today and a little tomorrow, and advancing its noiseless step like a thief over the field of jurisdiction until all shall be usurped from the States and the government be consolidated into one. To this I am opposed."* [6]

Article III also defines the term *"treason,"* which exists only when war is levied against the United States or when aid and comfort is given to an enemy of the United States. The limitations of this definition allow the federal judiciary to hear cases coming within the constitutional definition and also act as a safeguard to prohibit legislative or judicial creation of new treasons for which punishment could be rendered.

E. Article IV: Relations Between the States

Regulating peaceful relations between the states is an important function of the judiciary, as well as of the legislature. This Article consists of several sections that determine how controversies between and relationships among the states should be handled.

1. Article IV, section 1: Full Faith and Credit

The Constitution requires that full faith and credit be given in each state to *"the public Acts, Records, and judicial Proceedings of every other State."* This ensures that judicial decisions rendered by the courts in one state are recognized and honored in every other state. It also prevents parties from moving to another state to escape enforcement of a judgment or to re-litigate a controversy already decided elsewhere.

2. Article IV, section 2: Privileges and Immunities

The citizens of each state *"shall be entitled to all Privileges and Immunities of Citizens in the several States."* This section also provides for extradition of accused criminals from one state back to the state in which the crime was committed. Prior to the Civil War and the passage of the Thirteenth, Fourteenth and Fifteenth Amendments, the law allowed run-away slaves to be extradited for punishment back to the state where they had been enslaved. Following the abolition of slavery after the Civil War, this extradition provision no longer applied to former slaves, who were then able to enjoy the privileges and immunities of every other citizen in whichever state they chose to live.

3. Article IV, section 3: Admission of New States

New states can be admitted into the union subject to the following limitations: (1) no new state can be formed or erected within the jurisdiction of any other state; and (2) no state may be formed by the joining of two or more states, or parts of states, unless the particular state's legislature and the United States Congress consent. New states have been regularly admitted into the union, with the last two states, Alaska and Hawaii, having no common borders with the continental states. Both states were admitted into the Union in 1959.

The Constitution provides for the federal government to acquire and dispose of property, whether outside of the territorial United States or from within the several states. Article IV also guarantees the right of states to choose their own officers, to make their own laws, and to be protected by the federal government from invasion.

F. Article V: Amending the Constitution

The Founding Fathers realized that the Constitution would not address all future issues that might arise. Therefore, if the new nation were to survive and flourish, there had to be a formal means of amending the Constitution. The Founders provided two avenues for amending this document, neither of which involves the executive branch or the judiciary. These methods are as follows: (1) by congressional and state approval, and (2) by means of a constitutional convention.

Whenever two-thirds of both houses deem it necessary, Congress may propose amendments to the Constitution. Amendments proposed under this procedure are only valid after ratification by three-fourths of the states' legislatures. The fact that Congress proposes an amendment does not ensure its approval by the states.

If two-thirds of the states' legislatures request it, Congress may call a constitutional convention. Any Constitutional amendments proposed under this procedure are valid only when ratified by separate conventions in three-fourths of the states' legislatures.

G. Article VI: The Supremacy Clause and Oaths

This Article provides that the Constitution and the laws passed by Congress are the supreme law of the land, and federal law controls whenever federal and state laws conflict. It also provides for the assumption of debts entered into during the twelve years prior to the ratification of the Constitution (a provision that also recognized the previous existence of the union since the Declaration of Independence).

Article VI requires all U.S. Senators and Representatives, and "*all executive and judicial Officers, both of the United States and of the several States,*" to be bound "*by Oath or Affirmation to support this Constitution.*"

The Article says that "*no religious Test shall ever be required as a qualification to any Office or public Trust.*" Anti-religious commentators on the Constitution have sometimes argued that this prohibition of a "*no religious Test*" requirement proves that all religion must be separated from American political life. However, these commentators are wrong. This Test only means that no federal employee, whether elected or appointed, career or political, can be required to adhere to or accept any particular religion or belief. It does not mean that voters, candidates and legislators are required to check their faith at the door. This is made clear by the fact that every president since George Washington, with the sole exception of Thomas Jefferson, has taken the oath of office with his hand placed on the Bible and ending his oath with the words, "*So help me God,*" words which are not part of the prescribed constitutional oath of office. Furthermore, prayer is regularly offered in legislative bodies and presidents regularly end their speeches with "*God bless America.*" Given that these practices have endured for well over 200 years, it is clear that the "*no religious Test*" requirement was never intended to eliminate God from the operations of government officials.

H. Article VII: Ratification

Article VII requires that only nine states were needed to ratify the Constitution. This provision avoided the almost impossible requirement under the Articles of Confederation for all states to agree unanimously upon any action.

I. The Subscription Clause

> Done in convention by the unanimous consent of the States present on the seventeenth day of September in the year of our Lord one thousand seven hundred and eighty-seven and of the independence of the United States of America the twelfth. In witness whereof we have hereunto subscribed our names.

The Subscription Clause is important because it attested to the authenticity of the Constitution as signed by the majority of delegates to the Constitutional Convention. However, this clause is also important because its date connects the Constitution to the God of the Bible and the Christian foundations of America that are identified in the Declaration of Independence, which was issued twelve years earlier. The Subscription Clause declares that America was founded in 1776 with the Declaration of Independence, not upon the signing of the Constitution in 1787.

By embracing 1776 as the birthday of the nation, the Constitution signaled the incorporation of the Declaration of Independence by reference into the Constitution, including all of its foundational theological language and biblical principles. Rightfully understood, the Subscription Clause ties the Constitution to the Creator God of history. Those who argue to the contrary must specifically ignore the obvious meaning of the Subscription Clause.

This clause is also significant regarding the Christian history of America because our Founders fixed the date of their subscription according to the Gregorian calendar, which had been established during the reign of Pope Gregory XIII (1572-1585), or about two hundred years before the Constitution was written. The Gregorian calendar became known as the Christian calendar because it was anchored to the birth of Jesus. Significantly, from 1606 until 1752, England and her colonies had calculated time based on the Roman calendar, which was not tied to the birth of Jesus. At the time of the Revolution, England had only been using the Gregorian calendar for twenty-four years, yet when the Americans gained independence from England, they did not seek independence from the calendar that designated time from the birth of Christ.

On the other hand, the French Revolution, which occurred only a few years after the American Revolution, included a revolt against God as well as against the established political order. As a result, the French revolutionaries did not continue to follow the Gregorian calendar, but declared the year of their revolution to be Year One, even eliminating the seven-day theological week in favor of a more secularized ten-day week. The Americans did not revolt against God, but only against England, continuing to use the Gregorian calendar and the seven-day week with Sunday as the day of rest.

III. THE CALL FOR A BILL OF RIGHTS

The inclusion of a Bill of Rights in the United States Constitution was barely mentioned at the Philadelphia Constitutional Convention in 1787.

Most delegates saw it as unnecessary. They believed that the fundamental rights of individuals had been secured by the various individual state constitutions and that all power not expressly delegated to the new federal government was reserved to the people.

George Mason, however, did not agree. As one of seven Virginia delegates to the Constitutional Convention, Mason consistently spoke out in favor of the rights of individuals and against centralized governmental authority. Mason, the author of the Virginia Declaration of Rights, was convinced that *"there never was a government over a very extensive country without destroying the liberties of the people."*[7] His attempt at the Convention to include a Bill of Rights in the new Constitution was defeated by a unanimous vote of those present.

Although Mason stood nearly alone at the federal Constitutional Convention, his cry for a Bill of Rights was heeded at the state conventions when they were considering ratification of the Constitution. Mason's refusal to sign the Constitution without a Bill of Rights and his stated objections were published all over the country. Although he did not stop state ratification of the Constitution, he did cause many states to condition their approval on the understanding that Congress would immediately add a Bill of Rights. Mason's own state of Virginia was one of those states.

James Madison was elected as Virginia's delegate to the United States House of Representatives when the first Congress met in New York under the new federal Constitution. Although Madison did not personally see the necessity for a Bill of Rights in the Constitution, he did see the value in proposing such a bill. One of his goals was to pull in the two states— Rhode Island and North Carolina—that had yet to ratify the Constitution. Madison also recognized that a Bill of Rights would satisfy the states that had called for a declaration of rights during the ratification process. Madison expressed his view in these words:

> *[N]otwithstanding the ratification of this system of Government by eleven of the thirteen United States, . . .; yet still there is a great number of our constituents who are dissatisfied with it; among whom are many respectable for their talents and patriotism, and respectable for the jealousy they have for their liberty, which, though mistaken in its object, is laudable in its motive. . . We ought not to disregard their inclination, but, on principles of amity and moderation, conform to their wishes, and expressly declare the great rights of mankind secured under this constitution.*

The acquiescence which our fellow-citizens show under the Government, calls upon us for a like return of moderation.

I believe that the great mass of the people who opposed it, disliked it because it did not contain effectual provisions against encroachments on particular rights, and those safeguards which they have been long accustomed to have interposed between them and the magistrate who exercises the sovereign power; nor ought we to consider them safe, while a great number of our fellow-citizens think these securities necessary.[8]

In discussing the efficacy of a Bill of Rights with James Madison, Thomas Jefferson wrote on March 15, 1789:

The inconveniences of the Declaration are that it may cramp government in its useful exertions. But the evil of this is short-lived, moderate & reparable. The inconveniences of the want of a Declaration are permanent, afflicting & irreparable. They are in constant progression from bad to worse. The executive in our governments is not the sole, it is scarcely the principal object of my jealousy. The tyranny of the legislatures is the most formidable dread at present, and will be for long years. That of the executive will come in it's [sic] turn, but it will be at a remote period [NOTE: a period that America may now have reached.]. . . *I am much pleased with the prospect that a declaration of rights will be added.*[9]

In June 1789, James Madison introduced a Bill of Rights to the House of Representatives. Although Madison is credited as being the primary author, most of the Bill of Rights were drawn from the proposals made by Mason during the Constitutional Convention two years earlier. The original proposed Bill of Rights had twelve amendments; however, only ten were actually ratified by the states.

Madison's move in proposing a Bill of Rights to Congress also had the effect of neutralizing New York's call for another constitutional convention. Madison feared that another convention could result in the unraveling of the fledgling Constitution. He was successful in thwarting that initiative.

Eventually, Madison was also successful in persuading Congress to approve the proposed Bill of Rights. In doing so, he had to overcome arguments that it was premature to amend a Constitution that was as yet untested and, as a matter of priority, other important business should first be considered.

Nevertheless, Congress submitted a Bill of Rights with twelve amendments to the states for ratification on September 28, 1789. Two of the original twelve were not ratified by the states: one changing the apportionment of Congress and the other forbidding congressional pay raises to take effect until after the next election. [NOTE: In 1992, this latter proposal became the Twenty-seventh Amendment to the Constitution.]

IV. THE FEDERALIST PAPERS

After the Constitution was drafted in 1787, it had to be ratified by nine of the thirteen colonies before it could become the law of the land. Because New York was such a pivotal swing state in the approval process for the new Constitution, a series of anonymous, pro-Constitution letters began to appear in the newspapers there under the pseudonym *Publius*. These eighty-five letters to the editor came to be known as *The Federalist Papers* (sometimes called *The Federalist*). They help to shed light on what the Founders intended by the words of the Constitution, since they were written contemporaneously by those who had helped to frame that document.

The Federalist Papers should be required reading for all American students, but especially for law students, along with the Declaration of Independence and the Constitution. Most Americans are shocked to discover that these foundational documents are not required reading in most law schools! It is very disturbing to realize that many law students graduate, pass the bar exam, and begin to practice law without having even a vague understanding of the overarching biblical principles that formed our nation, its Constitution, and its laws.

The real identity of *Publius* was not known in 1789, but we know today that *The Federalist Papers* were written by Alexander Hamilton, James Madison, and John Jay. All three of these writers professed a strong faith in Jesus Christ. Their essays are still sometimes cited in legal briefs and quoted in various court decisions.

In *Federalist No. 15*, Alexander Hamilton, one of the authors, asked and answered the most basic civics question about man's sinful nature:

> *Why has government been instituted at all? Because the passions of men will not conform to the dictates of reason and justice without constraint.*

Federalist No. 55, which is generally attributed to either Hamilton or

Madison, discusses the necessity in a republican (or representative) form of government for both the electors and those elected to be of good character:

> *As there is a degree of depravity in mankind which requires a certain degree of circumspection and distrust, so there are other qualities in human nature which justify a certain portion of esteem and confidence. Republican government presupposes the existence of these qualities in a higher degree than any other form.*

Alexander Hamilton pointed out in *Federalist No. 22*:

> *The fabric of American empire ought to rest on the solid basis of THE CONSENT OF THE PEOPLE. The streams of national power ought to flow immediately from that pure, original fountain of all legitimate authority.*

The same thought was emphasized again in *Federalist No. 49*:

> *[T]he people are the only legitimate fountain of power, and it is from them that the constitutional charter, under which the several branches of government hold their power, is derived.*

By placing the authority of government in the consent of the governed, our Founders recognized that ultimately, through our representatives in the legislature, the majority—"we the people"—were to have the greater say. James Madison points out: "*In republican Government the majority however composed, ultimately give the law.*"

Today, in America, however, we have seen that when America's secularists do not have a sufficient majority to enact legislation favorable to them, they have taken an alternate route to establish their anti-God agenda through sympathetic judges, and ultimately through the United States Supreme Court, reinterpreting both our history and the Constitution itself. John Adams, a signer of the Declaration and our nation's second president, argued against such rule of men by affirming the superiority of a republic (where elected representatives make law) over a democracy (where a majority of people directly make the law), a nation of laws and not of men. He said:

> *There is no good government, but what is republican . . . [T]he very definition of a republic is "an empire of laws, and not of men." . . . [T]hat form of government which is best contrived to secure an*

impartial and exact execution of the laws, is the best of republics.
[10]

Most of the Founders were quite leery of the whole concept of a pure democracy, where the people hold all power directly to make the laws. Instead, the Founders established this nation as a republic, in which the government functions through elected representatives.

In *Federalist No. 10*, James Madison argued that the elected representatives of the people are able to administer government more wisely than the people themselves when acting as a pure democracy.[6] Colonial New England town meetings are one example where the people would gather to vote directly on proposed measures. He believed that a group of people acting directly would be more easily swayed by their passions toward factionalism than elected representatives, who would be more likely to apply their collective wisdom for the best interests of the country as a whole—so long as they were not given to temper, prejudice, or sinister designs.

One of the problems we see today in modern America, where the judiciary has assumed a greater power than originally assigned, is that factionalism has been magnified through partisan court appointments that lead to the political ascendancy of one unelected faction or another. The men who drafted the Constitution viewed the legislative branch as being far more important than the judicial branch. In fact, as the original Founders interpreted the Constitution, the judiciary was expected to be the least important branch of government. Article I of the Constitution (dealing with the legislature) received much more detailed attention than Article III (dealing with the judiciary). The Founding Fathers never intended for us to live under a "judge-ocracy," where the federal Supreme Court would rule as an oligarchy, remake the laws, and impose the will of the minority on the majority.

Alexander Hamilton pointed out in a footnote in *Federalist No. 78*: "*Of the three powers above mentioned, the judiciary is next to nothing.*" In the same Federalist, Hamilton discusses the constitutional dilemma that could arise were the judiciary to assert its will above the will of the people as expressed by the legislature. He concludes that the judiciary is not superior to the legislature, but is primarily "*to keep the latter within the limits assigned to their authority*" and to interpret the laws. However, he concludes that when

---

[6] A pure democracy is one in which the power to govern lies directly in the hands of the people rather than being exercised through their representatives.

a conflict develops, it is supposed that "*the power of the people is superior to both.*"

V. THE CONTINUING ROLE OF RELIGION IN ESTABLISHING GOOD GOVERNMENT

Our Founders understood that a constitutional government that placed ultimate power in the hands of the people would ultimately require a virtuous people in order to succeed. This is why the Black Regiment, the black-robed preachers who instructed their congregations from the pulpit every Sunday in both theology and politics, were expected to continue to play an important role in instructing the people in virtue.

Seven years before the United States Constitution was written, Massachusetts unveiled its state constitution. One of the influential members of the Black Regiment, Rev. Samuel Cooper of Boston, delivered a sermon in honor of that occasion (October 25, 1780) entitled "A Sermon on the Day of the Commencement of the Constitution." Rev. Cooper discussed the importance of virtue in maintaining good government:

[A]s piety and virtue support the honour and happiness of every community, they are peculiarly requisite in a free government. Virtue is the spirit of a republic; for where all power is derived from the people, all depends on their good disposition. If they are impious, factious and selfish; if they are abandoned to idleness, dissipation, luxury, and extravagance; if they are lost to the fear of God, and the love of their country, all is lost. Having got beyond the restraints of a divine authority, they will not brook the control of laws enacted by rulers of their own creating. We may therefore rely that the present government will do all it fairly can, by authority and example, to answer the end of its institution, that the members of this commonwealth may lead a quiet and peaceable life in all godliness as well as honesty, and our liberty never be justly reproached as licentiousness.[11]

Coming to the end of this sermon, Rev. Cooper predicted a great future for liberty if both government and citizens pursued a godly course: "*We seem called by heaven to make a large portion of this globe a seat of knowledge and liberty, of agriculture, commerce, and arts, and what is more important than all, of Christian piety and virtue.*"[12]

American Christians need to understand what is at stake today in our nation. Since the 1960s, because of various decisions by the United States Supreme Court favoring secularism over religion, America has begun to stray from its founding biblical principles. Some Americans now want to forget God's role in our nation's founding and history. Our citizens regularly break His laws and no longer think these Divine laws are important to our survival as a nation. Courts have jettisoned major portions of our Judeo-Christian heritage as unconstitutional. We must not forget what John Adams said about virtue being an implied assumption of our constitutional form of government. He warned his countrymen:

> *[W]e have no government armed with power capable of contending with human passions unbridled by morality and religion. Avarice, ambition, revenge, or gallantry, would break the strongest cords of our Constitution as a whale goes through a net. Our Constitution was made only for a moral and religious people. It is wholly inadequate to the government of any other.*[13]

VI. A CAUTIONARY NOTE

As great as the Constitution is, and as much as it was influenced by the Bible and by the godly men who wrote it, we must never put it on the same level as the Bible. The Bible itself should be the only source upon which Christians base their duties and responsibilities toward both God and government.

Some of the claims made by the Black Regiment during the Revolutionary War were exaggerated when they declared that the cause of America was the cause of Christ. Instead, President Abraham Lincoln reportedly struck a better chord when he pointed out during the Civil War that citizens should not so much ask whether the Lord is on their side, but rather, whether they are on the Lord's side.[14]

While American Christians must take great care to preserve the gifts of freedom and self-government that God has given to us, we must realize that it is God who raises up and tears down nations according to His sovereignty. Although no Christian should ever equate America with the Kingdom of God, as President Ronald Reagan was fond of saying, America is the *"last best hope of man on earth"*—primarily because it was founded on the unchanging Word of God.[15]

Chapter 7

The First Amendment Religion Clauses in The Bill of Rights

Some delegates to the Constitutional Convention would not agree to ratify the Constitution without a guarantee that a written Bill of Rights would be speedily enacted to secure religious freedom and other important individual liberties.

When the hard job of getting the states to ratify the new Constitution began, the first problem that surfaced was that many of the states, and even some of the delegates, would not agree to ratify the Constitution without a written Bill of Rights. Patrick Henry, Samuel Adams, and even Thomas Jefferson, who was thousands of miles away in France as our ambassador at the time, were among the many leaders of the founding era who insisted that the Constitution must clearly contain in writing those specific liberties the colonists were intent on preserving.

So, on September 25, 1789, three days after Congress authorized the appointment of paid chaplains, Congress drafted and enacted the first ten amendments to the Constitution, also known as the Bill of Rights, which include the First Amendment with its two important religion clauses: "*Congress shall make no law respecting an establishment of religion, or prohibiting the free exercise thereof.*" These two clauses are typically referred to as the Establishment Clause and the Free Exercise Clause. The first is a prohibition, while the second is a guarantee.

I. THE FIRST AMENDMENT FREEDOMS

Among the most important freedoms we enjoy as Americans are the freedoms of the First Amendment—freedom to associate and to petition the government, freedom of the press, and especially, the freedoms of religion and speech. Our Founding Fathers believed these rights were paramount to the survival of the new nation. Furthermore, they understood the importance of religion and virtue to the survival of our nation.

George Washington stated in his Farewell Address to the nation on leaving office in 1796, "*Of all the dispositions and habits which lead to political prosperity, Religion and morality are indispensable supports.*" John Adams recognized, "*Our Constitution was made only for a moral and religious people. . . . It is wholly inadequate to the government of any other.*"[1] Finally, Charles Carroll of Maryland, signer of the Declaration of Independence, remarked, "*Without morals a republic cannot subsist any length of time; they therefore who are decrying the Christian religion whose morality is so sublime and pure . . . are undermining the solid foundation of morals, the best security for the duration of free governments.*"[2]

The First Amendment's freedom of religion guarantee is divided by courts into two clauses: the Establishment Clause and the Free Exercise Clause. Each is treated differently by our modern courts and, therefore, each will be discussed separately.

II. BAPTIST INFLUENCE ON THE FIRST AMENDMENT RELIGION CLAUSES

For two decades prior to the American Revolution, Baptists endured severe religious persecution, particularly in the Anglican colony of Virginia. In Virginia at that time, Baptist pastors were beaten, arrested, and whipped for the offense of proclaiming the Gospel. "*The Baptists, on the one hand were to be severely persecuted for their religious fidelity, and on the other hand were to play a key role in the ultimate fight for religious freedom.*"[3] Various Baptist histories document the extreme suffering and persecution endured by the Baptists from 1765 and 1778, stories of which encouraged men like Thomas Jefferson and James Madison to call for religious liberty. Before Jefferson's Act for Establishing Religious Freedom was enacted by the Virginia legislature in 1786, faithful Baptists, and particularly Baptist preachers, suffered greatly.[4] Thomas Jefferson of Virginia stood boldly against such religious oppression. In 1781 he wrote:

Millions of innocent men, women, and children, since the introduction of Christianity, have been burnt, tortured, fined, imprisoned; yet we have not advanced one inch towards uniformity. What has been the effect of coercion? To make one half the world fools, and the other half hypocrites. To support roguery and error all over the earth. Let us reflect that it is inhabited by a thousand millions of people. That these profess probably a thousand different systems of religion. That ours is but one of that thousand. That if there be but one right, and ours that one, we should wish to see the 999 wandering sects gathered into the fold of truth. But against such a majority we cannot effect this by force. Reason and persuasion are the only practicable instruments. To

*make way for these, free enquiry must be indulged; and how can
we wish others to indulge it while we refuse it ourselves.*[5]

Jefferson's *Virginia Act for Establishing Religious Freedom (1786)* was
supported by the Baptist General Association and provided for religious
freedom. The Act said:

> *[N]o man shall be compelled to frequent or support any religious
> worship, place, or ministry whatsoever, nor shall be enforced,
> restrained, molested, or [burdened] in his body or goods, nor shall
> otherwise suffer, on account of his religious opinions or belief; but
> that all men shall be free to profess, and by argument to maintain,
> their opinions in matters of religion, and that the same shall in no
> wise diminish, enlarge, or affect their civil capacities.*

It comes as no surprise, therefore, that Baptists in Virginia were unwilling
to approve the federal Constitution without a similar guarantee of religious
liberty. John Leland, the most prominent Virginia Baptist preacher at the
time of the Revolution, took the lead in this struggle for religious freedom.
An itinerant preacher who traveled thousands of miles and preached
thousands of sermons, Leland believed religious liberty was an unalienable
right and not a favor granted by any government.[6]

James Madison disappointed Virginia Baptists when he opposed adding a
Bill of Rights to the U.S. Constitution. Madison was satisfied that section 3
of Article VI provided for religious liberty, namely that: "*No religious Test
shall ever be required as a qualification to any Office or public trust under
the United States.*" John Leland had the opposite opinion as shown in his
writings:

> *What is clearest of all—Religious Liberty, is not sufficiently
> secured, No Religious test is Required as a qualification to fill any
> office under the United States, but if a Majority of Congress with
> the President favour one System more then another, they may
> oblige all others to pay to the support of their System as much
> as they please, and if Oppression does not ensue, it will be owing
> to the Mildness of Administration and not to any Constitutional
> defence, and of the Manners of People are so far Corrupted, that
> they cannot live by Republican principles, it is Very Dangerous
> leaving Religious Liberty at their Mercy.*[7]

As a result, tradition says that Leland was preparing to oppose Madison
as the Orange County candidate to the 1788 Virginia Convention called

to ratify the Constitution. Leland would have been a formidable candidate for Madison. He was an esteemed leader among the burgeoning Baptist population of Virginia and had the support of the Virginia Baptist General Committee. After a six-year revival, Baptists had become the most populous sect in the state; and it would have been impossible for Madison to win without their support.

However, Madison and Leland chose to hash out their differences privately instead of at the ballot box. There is good historical evidence to show that Madison and Leland met at Fredericksburg in March of 1788. It is said that in return for Leland withdrawing from the race and throwing Baptist support to Madison, Madison agreed to support a Bill of Rights that would include freedom of religion after the Constitution was adopted.[8]

Madison knew the importance of satisfying Baptist voters in Virginia. He knew that without Baptist support he would not be a delegate at Virginia's ratifying convention; but even worse, Virginia would not ratify the Constitution. He feared the domino effect this could have on other states. Both Madison and Leland were true to their word. Leland encouraged Baptists to support Madison in the election, and Madison introduced the First Amendment as part of the Bill of Rights in Congress on June 7, 1789.

Although Madison's support for the First Amendment was politically motivated, his writings make clear that he stood against the tyranny of religious persecution. He was an ardent supporter of religious liberty. For example, in 1785, he opposed a general tax for the support of teachers of the Christian religion. In his *Memorial and Remonstrance* he wrote these words in opposition to the tax:

> 1. *Because we hold it for a fundamental and undeniable truth, "that religion or the duty which we owe to our Creator and the manner of discharging it, can be directed only by reason and conviction, not by force or violence." The Religion then of every man must be left to the conviction and conscience of every man; and it is the right of every man to exercise it as these may dictate. This right is in its nature an unalienable right. . .*

> 2. *. . . Who does not see that the same authority which can establish Christianity, in exclusion of all other Religions, may establish with the same ease any particular sect of Christians, in exclusion of all other Sects? that the same authority which can force a citizen to contribute three pence only of his property for*

the support of any one establishment, may force him to conform to any other establishment in all cases whatsoever?

3. . . . Whilst we assert for ourselves a freedom to embrace, to profess and to observe the Religion which we believe to be of divine origin, we cannot deny an equal freedom to those whose minds have not yet yielded to the evidence which has convinced us. If this freedom be abused, it is an offence against God, not against man: To God, therefore, not to man, must an account of it be rendered. . .

11. . . . Torrents of blood have been spilt in the old world by vain attempts of the secular arm to extinguish religious discord by proscribing all difference in religious opinion. Time has at length revealed the true remedy. Every relaxation of narrow and rigorous policy, wherever it has been tried, has been found to assuage the disease. The American Theatre has exhibited proofs that equal and compleat liberty, if it does not wholly eradicate it, sufficiently destroys its malignant influence on the health and prosperity of the State. If with the salutary effects of this system under our own eyes, we begin to contract the bounds of Religious freedom, we know no name that will too severely reproach our folly. . .

The integrity of James Madison and John Leland, along with their conviction and strong leadership, were crucial elements in the passage of the religion clauses in the First Amendment.

III. THE ESTABLISHMENT CLAUSE AND THE SEPARATION OF CHURCH AND STATE

The Establishment Clause of the First Amendment states that "*Congress shall make no law respecting an establishment of religion . . . .*" The framer's intention was to forbid the federal government from establishing an official state church, such as the Church of England. However, since the Supreme Court's decision in *Everson v. Bd. of Education*, 330 U.S. 1 (1947), with a court-imposed "separation of church and state" legal doctrine, this clause has been used by courts all over the United States to silence Christianity and impose an entirely secularist philosophy that does not equally honor the basic Judeo-Christian foundations of America.

It should be carefully noted that the First Amendment says absolutely nothing about "the separation of church and state." In fact, that phrase is found nowhere in the Constitution or in the Bill of Rights. This doctrine of "separation" did not enter American jurisprudence until the *Everson* decision, nearly two hundred years after the Clause was drafted. The decision in the *Everson* case, which involved bus transportation to Catholic schools, was written by Justice Hugo Black, a former anti-Catholic Klansman.

Although now often distorted in modern court decisions, this now infamous phrase was first used in 1802 by President Thomas Jefferson. He wrote these words in an exchange of letters with the Baptist Association of Danbury, Connecticut, in order to assure the Baptists that the government would never be permitted to interfere with the church. Yet, against all reasonable interpretation, this phrase from a letter written by a man who took no part in the drafting of the First Amendment, has been seized upon by our courts since 1947 to deny citizens many of the rights that were once understood to be protected under our Constitution.

The Founders' own understanding of the Establishment Clause does not support the modern view of a complete church-state separation, which is really interpreted by modern courts to mean that the God of the Bible must be stricken completely from government. What the Founders themselves meant by *"an establishment of religion"* in the First Amendment was simply that there should be no officially established national church which citizens would be forced to attend and financially support, as there had been in England.

James Madison's original draft of the religion clauses shows his view concerning the "separation of church and state:"

> *The Civil rights of none shall be abridged on account of religious belief or worship, nor shall any national religion be established, nor shall the full and equal rights of conscience be in any manner, or on any pretext, infringed.*[9]

IV. JEFFERSON AND THE DANBURY BAPTISTS

In 1801, the Danbury Baptist Association in the state of Connecticut rejoiced at the election of Thomas Jefferson as the third President of the United States. On October 7 they wrote to Jefferson, a fellow believer in religious liberty, saying: *"[We] believe that America's God has raised you up to fill the Chair of State."* The Danbury Baptists complained to Jefferson of religious laws made by Connecticut's government. They feared the Congregational Church would become the state-sponsored religion and expressed approval for Jefferson's refusal to *"assume the prerogative of Jehovah and make laws to govern the Kingdom of Christ."* Although the Danbury Baptists understood that Jefferson, as president, could not *"destroy the laws of each State,"* they expressed hope that his sentiment would affect the states *"like the radiant beams of the sun."*[10]

It was Jefferson's response to this letter that is the origin of the infamous phrase "separation of church and state" used in the 1947 *Everson* decision. Jefferson's reply on January 1, 1802, showed his agreement with the Danbury Baptists that:

> *Religion is a matter which lies solely between man and his God, that he owes account to none other for his faith or his worship, that the legislative powers of government reach actions only, and not opinions, I contemplate with sovereign reverence that act of the whole American people which declared that their legislature should "make no law respecting an establishment of religion, or prohibiting the free exercise thereof," thus building a wall of separation between Church and State.*[11]

In referring to this *"wall of separation,"* Jefferson was borrowing from the metaphor of Roger Williams, a fellow Baptist and Rhode Island's champion of religious freedom. Williams had previously written of "*a gap in the hedge or wall of separation between the garden of the church and the wilderness of the world.*"

Christian scholars interpret Jefferson's Danbury letter in its context. They accept Jefferson's view that religion is a personal matter that should not be regulated by the federal government and that the federal government has no power to change law in the states. They interpret the "wall of separation" in the same way Roger Williams did: as a wall to protect God's garden from the world, to protect the church from the government.

In contrast, secularist scholars have lifted the Danbury letter out of its historical context. They turn the "wall" metaphor on its head and now use it to ostensibly protect the government from the church, establishing a freedom *from* religion not known by the Founders. This results in a concerted effort to rid government of any religious influence. Hence, we have the opposition to such things as Bible reading in schools, official proclamations promoting religious events, nativity scenes in public displays, the posting of the Ten Commandments in and on public buildings, prayer in public places, etc. These secular scholars fail to recognize that the

Danbury Baptists would never have rejoiced at Jefferson's election if he stood for a removal of religious influence on the government.

In *Everson*, the decision that gave the "wall" metaphor constitutional standing, Justice Black, writing the Court's majority opinion, said:

> *The First Amendment has erected a wall between church and state. That wall must be kept high and impregnable. We could not approve the slightest breach.*

It is interesting to note that no breach of the wall was actually found in *Everson*. The New Jersey statute permitting the state to reimburse parents for the expense of busing their children to and from private parochial schools was upheld as constitutional. The Court merely used this decision to introduce a new legal principle ("separation of church and state") that would later be employed in a modern attempt to completely separate God from government.

The *Everson* decision is a clear departure from the views of Thomas Jefferson and the Founding Fathers. The First Amendment was not intended to stop the states from establishing a church or from locally favoring a particular majority religion. Both Jefferson and the Danbury Baptists understood this. Jefferson's reference to the legislature of *"the whole American people"* demonstrates his understanding that the First Amendment applied to the federal government exclusively. Indeed, on January 23, 1808, Thomas Jefferson wrote to Rev. Samuel Miller:

> *Certainly no power to prescribe any religious exercise, or to assume authority in religious discipline, has been delegated to the general government. It must then rest with the states, as far as it can be in any human authority.*[12]

The Danbury Baptists did not even ask Jefferson to apply the First Amendment to the states. They acknowledged, *"The national government cannot destroy the laws of each State;"* rather, they looked to Jefferson's power of persuasion to prevail in Connecticut.

In the ongoing legal odyssey to find the true meaning of the "wall of separation between church and state," it is useful to consider the actions of the Founders after the First Amendment was passed. Reviewing a sampling of their activities makes it clear that the Founders had no intention of neutralizing government from all religious influence:

- The House of Representatives called for a national day of prayer and thanksgiving on September 24, 1789—the same day that it passed the First Amendment.

- From 1789 to today, Congress has authorized chaplains, paid by public funds, to offer prayers in Congress and in the armed services.

- Jefferson closed the Danbury letter, written in his official capacity as president, with a Judeo-Christian prayer: *"I reciprocate your kind prayers for the protection and blessing of the common Father and Creator of man."*

- On the very day Jefferson sent his letter to the Danbury Baptists he was making plans to attend church services in the House of Representatives.[13]

- Jefferson signed a treaty into law in 1803 that provided for a government-funded Christian missionary to the Kaskaskia Indians.[14]

- In response to a congressional request on July 9, 1812, President James Madison issued a proclamation recommending a day of public humiliation and prayer to be observed by the people of the United States, with religious solemnity.[15]

- In 1832 and 1833, Congress approved land grants to Columbian College (later George Washington University) and Georgetown University Baptist and Jesuit schools respectively. [16] [17]

- The Ten Commandments are inscribed on the wall of the United States Supreme Court.

- The Supreme Court begins each session with the prayer: *"God save the United States and this Honorable Court."*

- The New England Primer was used in public schools despite its many Judeo-Christian religious references.

- Every president has invoked God's name or the equivalent in a prayerful manner in his inaugural address.

The views of our first couple presidents on matters of church and state also challenge the viewpoint of our modern courts with regard to a separation of God and government:

> *Of all the dispositions and habits which lead to political prosperity, religion and morality are indispensable supports . . . And let us with caution indulge the supposition that morality can be maintained without religion. . .reason and experience both forbid us to expect that national morality can prevail in exclusion of religious principle. It is substantially true, that virtue or morality is a necessary spring of popular government.*
> —*George Washington, Farewell Address to the United States, 1796*

> *In matters of religion I have considered that its free exercise is placed by the Constitution independent of the powers of the General Government. I have therefore undertaken on no occasion to prescribe the religious exercises suited to it, but have left them, as the Constitution found them, under the direction and discipline of the church or state authorities acknowledged by the several religious societies.*
> —*Thomas Jefferson, Second Inaugural Address, March 4, 1805*

The intent of the First Amendment and the words and actions of our Founding Fathers, including Thomas Jefferson, clearly demonstrate how "the separation of church and state" was originally understood by the Founders. These words were never intended to remove God from government; rather they were intended to keep government from controlling and manipulating private religious practices. Unfortunately today, more than two hundred years after Jefferson used the phrase, courts have turned these words against those they were intended to protect.

V. APPLICATION OF THE ESTABLISHMENT CLAUSE UNDER THE FOURTEENTH AMENDMENT

In the *Everson* case, discussed previously, the Supreme Court also held for the first time that the Establishment Clause of the First Amendment applied to individual states through the Due Process Clause of the Fourteenth Amendment. This is called the "incorporation doctrine." Prior to this ruling, only the federal government was constitutionally precluded from establishing a religion.

The Court held in *Everson* that neither the state nor the federal government may constitutionally set up a church, nor pass laws that aid one religion, aid all religions, or prefer one religion over another. The Court claimed that Jefferson's high wall of separation between church and state was constitutionally mandated, but this decision, coming nearly two hundred years after the Religion Clauses had been drafted, marked the Court's first discovery of this concept of a constitutionally mandated complete separation between God and government. It is this Supreme Court incorporation of the Establishment Clause applied to individual states and local governments that now stands in the way of individual states and localities enacting legislation that recognizes the majority religion of the people. Were it not for this incorporation, local school districts could still permit prayers in public school absent a state law to the contrary.

The Supreme Court's assault against religion began in 1947. Since then, the Court has continued to use this interpretation of the Establishment Clause, which our Founders would not recognize, to curb religious freedom in public schools, as well as in other areas of public life. One year later, in *McCollum v. Bd. of Education*, 333 U.S. 203 (1948), the Court used the Establishment Clause to strike down voluntary religion classes in public schools, even when parental permission was required before a student could attend.

In the early 1960s, the Supreme Court began using the Establishment Clause to further restrict religious freedom in public schools. In *Engel v. Vitale*, 370 U.S. 421 (1962), the Court invoked the Establishment Clause to strike down prayer in the public schools, even when the prayer was both voluntary and nondenominational.

In 1963, the Supreme Court found Bible reading in the schools to be unconstitutional in the case of *School District of Abington Township v. Schempp*, 374 U.S. 203 (1963). In *Epperson v. Arkansas*, 393 U.S. 97 (1968), the Court struck down a 40-year-old state statute that had prohibited teaching Darwinian evolution in public schools. Evolution is now something public schools generally mandate.

In one of its more outrageous decisions, the Supreme Court in *Stone v. Graham*, 449 U.S. 39 (1980), found a display of the Ten Commandments in the public schools to be unconstitutional. The Court explained:

> *If the posted copies of the Ten Commandments are to have any effect at all, it will be to induce the school children to read,*

meditate upon, perhaps to venerate and obey, the Commandments. However desirable this might be as a matter of private devotion, it is not a permissible state objective under the Establishment Clause.

In 1992, in the case of *Lee v. Weisman*, 505 U.S. 577 (1992), the Supreme Court struck down clerical invocations and benedictions offered at graduation ceremonies. Some legal analysts see the Court's decision in the *Lee* case as a watershed moment in the Supreme Court's continuing expression of hostility toward religion. In *Lee*, the Court viewed a simple non-sectarian invocation offered by a Rabbi as somehow coercive, dangerous, and harmful to children. Some lower courts have since permitted prayers at graduation if given by students.

In 2000, in the case of *Santa Fe v. Doe*, 530 U.S. 290 (2000), the Supreme Court determined that prayers offered by students before football games were unconstitutional because a school policy encouraged the practice and provided a microphone for the students. It appears that a majority of Supreme Court Justices have become hostile and paranoid about even the simplest and most general religious expression in public schools, despite the fact that the Free Exercise of Religion is the second balancing clause in the First Amendment's religious freedom protections.

VI. IMPLEMENTATION OF THE *LEMON* TEST TO FIND ESTABLISHMENT CLAUSE VIOLATIONS

The *Lemon* test was developed by the Supreme Court in a 1971 decision, *Lemon v. Kurtzman*, 403 U.S. 602 (1971), to determine whether a particular law violated the Establishment Clause. The dispute in *Lemon* concerned the constitutionality of a law in Pennsylvania that provided secular textbooks to parochial schools and a law in Rhode Island that provided state salary supplements to teachers in religious schools who taught non-religious subjects. Both laws were declared unconstitutional. Under the *Lemon* test, a public religious activity is upheld as constitutional only if it (1) has a predominantly secular purpose; (2) neither inhibits nor advances religion; and (3) creates no excessive entanglement between government and religion.

There have been some positive Supreme Court decisions that protect religious liberties. One such notable case that did use the *Lemon* test was *Lynch v. Donnelly*, 465 U.S. 668 (1984), where the Court upheld the display of a government-owned nativity scene in Rhode Island, finding that the city had met all three prongs of the *Lemon* test. However, positive outcomes are more likely to result when the Court uses a test that requires equal treatment for everyone regardless of their religious or non-religious viewpoint rather than a strict *Lemon* test. For example, in *Westside v. Mergens*, 496 U.S. 226 (1990), the Court upheld a federal equal access law stating that schools must allow equal access to school buildings for both religious and non-religious student groups.

In *Lamb's Chapel v. Center Moriches*, 508 U.S. 384 (1993), the Court overturned a school board decision prohibiting the after-school use of school property by a church when it had previously allowed non-religious groups to use the property for similar purposes. In *Zobrest v. Catalina Foothills*, 509 U.S. 1 (1993), the Court upheld a law that authorized the use of a publicly-funded sign language interpreter for a deaf student attending a religious school. In 1995, the Court in *Rosenberger v. University of Virginia*, 515 U.S. 819 (1995), ruled that a university must reimburse publishing costs to a religious student group the same as it reimbursed printing costs for non-religious student groups out of the student activity fees. Despite these positive outcomes, this area of law continues to lack any clear standards for predicting how the Court might rule in any given religion case.

VII. FREEDOM OF RELIGION UNDER THE FREE EXERCISE CLAUSE

In addition to addressing the Establishment of Religion, the First Amendment Religion Clauses also provide that Congress shall not "*prohibit the free exercise*" of religion. Theoretically, this provision means that the government cannot punish or disadvantage a person based upon that person's religious beliefs. While the freedom to *believe* whatever one desires continues to be absolutely protected in America, the Free Exercise Clause has not been interpreted to allow that same level of protection for *conduct* based on religious belief.

This interpretation began with the Supreme Court's decision in *Reynolds v. U.S.*, 98 U.S. 145 (1879). The *Reynolds* case involved the right of the government to make bigamy a crime in federal territories. Mormon religious advocates claimed that polygamy was their religious duty and, therefore, the practice should not be criminalized. The United States Supreme Court held that conduct that violates a law is not justifiable simply because a religious practice commands it. In other words, while the Mormons had the right to believe as they wished, they did not have the right to live out that belief as a "Free Exercise" right if their conduct violated a law, so long as that law had not been passed for the purpose of burdening religion. This decision, in effect, limited the Free Exercise Clause to mean that a person has the right to believe as one wishes in accordance with his religion, not to act as one wishes.

The Free Exercise Clause, as with the entire Bill of Rights, was initially intended only to restrict certain actions by the federal government, not the states. The Free Exercise Clause was first applied to the states, as well as to the federal government, in the case of *Cantwell v. Connecticut*, 310 U.S. 296 (1940). *Cantwell* involved the conviction of several Jehovah's Witnesses for proselytizing in the streets without a license in a manner that provoked their hearers to anger. The Court overturned their convictions and declared that giving government officials the discretion to require a license in order to engage in religious speech is unconstitutional. But the Court also noted, as it had in *Reynolds*, that while the freedom to believe is absolute, the freedom to act on those beliefs is not always absolute. The *Cantwell* case was the first time the Court used the incorporation doctrine to apply the Free Exercise Clause to state or local, as well as federal, matters.

Despite the ruling in favor of the Jehovah's Witnesses, the *Cantwell* decision did not provide a basis for total freedom to exercise religious expression. In fact, courts today will not protect a person's right to the "Free Exercise of Religion" unless the court also determines there was a second First Amendment freedom (such as Freedom of Speech or Freedom of Assembly) violated during the same incident that brought about the alleged free exercise violation. The Supreme Court articulated this principle in the 1990 case of *Employment Division v. Smith*, 494 U.S. 872, when it issued a decision upholding an Oregon law that criminalized the use of peyote, which Native Americans had argued was protected by their free exercise of religion. The Supreme Court said that where a law criminalizes conduct or actions that a particular religion considers part of its "religious expression" (like using the illegal drug peyote for religious reasons), persons can be found guilty of violating that law unless one of two scenarios exist. First, if the legislature has provided for a religious exemption under that law, then the behavior/conduct is permitted for those to whom the exemption applies. Second, if there is no religious exemption, the behavior/conduct can only be protected as a legitimate free exercise of religion if a second First Amendment violation also resulted from the incident. In other words, courts will not find a violation of the Free Exercise Clause alone- it must be combined with some other recognized constitutional right before it will be protected by the court. Justice Scalia, writing for the majority, called this a "hybrid situation." The effect of this decision is that the Free Exercise Clause is now the only First Amendment right that cannot stand alone as a constitutionally guaranteed protection.

Prior to the *Smith* decision, courts had used different standards to protect freedom of religious expression (referred to in the Constitution as "free exercise"). These standards for determining the justification of government regulations that burden religion were articulated in *Sherbert v. Verner*, 374 U.S. 398 (1963) and *Wisconsin v. Yoder*, 406 U.S. 205 (1972). Both of these cases understood the right to the "Free Exercise of Religion" to be a stand-alone right, a determination the Court no longer recognized after *Smith*.

In *Sherbert v. Verner*, 374 U.S. 398 (1963), the Court set forth a two-part test. First, judges must consider whether the law being reviewed places a substantial burden on the free exercise of the person's religion. Second, the court must consider whether there is a "compelling state interest" that would outweigh this burden. If the court finds that there is a substantial burden but no compelling state interest, the law will be overturned. On the other hand, if the court finds there is a compelling state interest even in a law that substantially burdens religion, that law may be upheld. The *Sherbert* "compelling state interest" test thus became the standard of review used in free exercise cases beginning in 1963.

In the 1972 case of *Wisconsin v. Yoder*, 406 U.S. 205 (1972), however, the Court moved away from the "compelling state interest" language used in *Sherbert*, in favor of applying a simpler "balancing test" to balance the interests of free exercise of religion against the compelling interest of the government in enacting laws that might burden religious expression. In *Yoder*, the issue was whether the state could require the children of Amish parents to attend public schools beyond the eighth grade in violation of their religious beliefs. The Court struck down the law, and in the process set forth the following two-part balancing test: (1) does the law place a burden on the exercise of religion; and (2) if so, that burden must then be weighed against the importance of the state interest found in the regulation.

The Supreme Court has never overturned *Sherbert* or *Yoder*. Instead, the Court specifically stated in the *Smith* decision that both the *Sherbert* and *Yoder* cases had been the type of "hybrid situation" the Court was now requiring in *Smith*. Nevertheless, the *Smith* decision had the practical negative impact of declaring the Free Exercise Clause to be the only First Amendment freedom that must be combined with some other recognized constitutional right before it can be protected by the courts.

Following the *Smith* decision, Congress passed the 1993 RFRA (Religious Freedom Restoration Act) in order to restore the previous *Sherbert/Yoder* standard as a stand-alone protection for religious free exercise. Under RFRA, if a generally applicable law (a law that applies to everyone, regardless of their religion) substantially burdened the free exercise of religion, the government would be required to have a compelling reason to enforce that law and would need to show that the law was the "least restrictive" way to accomplish the compelling public interest.

By enacting RFRA, Congress recognized that religious freedom could be threatened by generally applicable laws as well as by laws that specifically target religion if the law did not specifically provide for a religious exemption. One example of a general law that could negatively affect religious free exercise is a state or local law forbidding the wearing of hats in a public building. In enforcing that general law, a conservative Jewish person would also be forbidden to wear a yarmulke in the public building unless the legislation provided a specific exemption for religion. Another example would be a general zoning law prohibiting the establishment of schools in certain sections of a city. Such a law would not specifically target religion because no one, whether religious or not, could have a school in that area. If a church were already established in that section of a city, however, that church could not open a Christian school in that building unless churches were specifically exempted from the law. If the law did not provide an exemption and if the government did not have a compelling reason for refusing an exemption, then a court could protect religious free exercise for the Jewish person and the church-school under RFRA.

Despite Congress's efforts to get around the effect *Smith* had on religious free exercise, trouble lay ahead for RFRA. In 1997, the United States Supreme Court declared in *City of Boerne v. Flores*, 521 U.S. 507 (1997), that RFRA could apply only to federal laws, not to state or local laws. This decision once again put the status of religious free exercise in America in jeopardy. The issue in the *Boerne* case was that a church in Boerne, Texas, had been prevented from enlarging its building under local zoning laws intended to preserve historical landmarks. The church challenged the law under the principles of RFRA.

The Court held that the local historic preservation law in Boerne, Texas was appropriately applied to the church because the federal RFRA law was unconstitutional when applied to state or local laws. As a result of this case, individual states were now required to enact their own state RFRAs in order to protect the free exercise of religion on a state-by-state basis. Since that 1997 *Boerne* decision, many states have enacted state RFRAs and all states should do so in order to protect religious free exercise standing on its own.

Following *Boerne*, Congress attempted again to protect religious expression nationwide by enacting the Religious Land Use and Institutionalized Persons Act of 2000 (RLUIPA). RLUIPA specifically protects religious expression in areas of land use and protects religious liberty for institutionalized persons, such as prisoners. While RLUIPA has also come under constitutional attack in the courts, it has not been declared unconstitutional by the United States Supreme Court.

Congress, states, and local governments may enact additional laws specifically designed to protect freedom of religion within their own jurisdictions. One such federal law is the 1998 Religious Liberty and Charitable Donation Protection Act passed by Congress to limit a bankruptcy trustee's power to collect the tithes donated by bankrupt Christians as much as a year before they filed for bankruptcy.

This area of religious free exercise law remains confusing as modern courts are tending to move our society away from its constitutional foundation in the Judeo-Christian religious tradition. Our Founders made religious liberty America's First Freedom in the Bill of Rights. It now appears, however, to have become the least protected freedom.

In *Smith*, the Supreme Court passed the ball of religious free exercise protection to legislatures to provide religious exemptions for laws that are neutral towards religion on their face but that may still impact a person's religious exercise (such as the "no hats in public buildings" discussion above). Therefore, citizens must demand that legislatures place exemptions for religious belief in all generally applicable laws that might negatively impact the free exercise of religion.

In order for a legislative exemption strategy to be successful in protecting our rights of religious expression, Christians must become active participants in the political process at all levels. There are many areas of political influence where Christians can become involved: on the local school board; in local, state or federal legislative bodies; and in jurisdictions where judges are elected. While not every Christian can run for office, each one can play a part in assisting those candidates who are positively inclined to protect religious liberties.

Although Christians must pay close attention to the political process in order to protect free exercise rights, we must also remember that God is clearly still on the throne. He is never surprised by man's actions. As we are told in Proverbs 21:1: *"The king's heart is in the hand of the LORD, as the rivers of water: he turneth it whithersoever he will."*

Chapter 8

First Amendment Freedom of Speech and Its Impact on Religion

Christians have retained more rights under the
First Amendment doctrine of Free Speech than
under the First Amendment Religion Clauses.

The Supreme Court, in *Reynolds*, made a clear distinction between protecting religious belief and protecting religious conduct. This is a problem for Christians, given that Christianity is more than merely a set of religious beliefs; it is primarily a way of life, a manner of conduct. When the Declaration of Independence was written, the Founders understood this, and based our liberties, including our religious liberties, on our duties to the Creator God of the Bible. Those duties are thus what dictate our conduct as Christians. Given the *Reynolds* decision, and other negative court interpretations of the First Amendment Religion Clauses since the mid-20th century that tend to protect religious belief more than religious conduct, Christians have generally been more successful in protecting their religious rights by using the First Amendment Free Speech Clause. Occasionally, the First Amendment Freedom of Assembly Clause has also been used to protect the religious rights of Christians, particularly when groups of Christians are involved. Unfortunately, however, even the right of Free Speech is not absolute when it comes to defending religious liberties.

I. PROTECTION OF SPEECH IN TRADITIONAL PUBLIC FORUMS

The Supreme Court has held that in order to regulate speech in traditional public forums (such as streets and parks), the government must use the least restrictive means of achieving legitimate government objectives. Furthermore, if the government tries to prohibit speech based on the speaker's content or viewpoint alone, the state bears the burden of showing a compelling justification for such an infringement. Generally, government controls over content and viewpoint are disfavored and are struck down by the Court, particularly in traditional public forum areas or in areas the government has designated as being compatible with free speech. The first case articulating these principles was *Hague v. CIO*, 307 U.S. 496 (1939).

II. TIME, PLACE, AND MANNER RESTRICTIONS ON SPEECH

Restrictions on the time, place, or manner of speech are generally upheld so long as they are content neutral,[7] provide for adequate communication to the target audience, are the least restrictive means available to accomplish the government's legitimate purpose, and are not vague or overbroad or allow too much discretion on the part of government officials. This means that the government may regulate speech by means of any reasonable time, place, and manner restriction so long as the government leaves a workable alternative for the speaker to get out his message. Because of these requirements, time, place, and manner regulations must be narrowly tailored and may not be substantially broader than necessary to achieve a significant government interest (*Ward v. Rock Against Racism*, 491 U.S. 781 (1989)).

III. DISCRETION OF PUBLIC OFFICIALS IN GRANTING LICENSES TO SPEAK

Free speech protections also mandate that public officials not be given overly broad discretion to grant or deny permits or licenses without clearly articulated standards (*Freedman v. Maryland*, 380 U.S. 51 (1965)). When officials are given unbridled authority to determine who can and cannot speak without very specific guidelines, the courts view such authority, in essence, as content or viewpoint control, and such laws are routinely struck down as unconstitutional (*Forsyth Cnty. v. Nationalist Movement*, 505 U.S. 123 (1992); *Lakewood v. Plain Dealer Publ'g Co.*, 486 U.S. 750 (1988)).

IV. PROTECTIONS GRANTED TO LITERATURE DISTRIBUTION

In the interest of protecting free speech, the Supreme Court long ago decided that an ordinance may not prohibit all distribution of literature (*Lovell v. Griffin*, 303 U.S. 444 (1938)). This type of ordinance is unconstitutionally overbroad because it sweeps within its coverage speech and conduct that is protected by the speech guarantees of the First Amendment. As such, this type of ordinance is a violation of freedom of speech.

For purposes of constitutional analysis, written and oral speech receive comparable First Amendment protection. Furthermore, religious speech, including prayer and proselytizing, has generally been considered to fall

---

[7] Content neutral laws refer generally to laws that are without bias, and treat all views, including religious views, the same.

within the speech that the Free Speech clause is intended to protect. The assumption that this is true, however, is coming under attack by some federal government regulations and military policies that have sought to make a distinction between proselytizing (which, they claim, can be prohibited because of its harassing nature) and other constitutionally protected religious speech. Religious proselytizing has always been protected free speech in America and should continue to be so.

V. TYPES OF SPEECH SUBJECT TO CONSTITUTIONALLY VALID RESTRAINT

Another guarantee under the First Amendment Free Speech clause is that speech may not be prohibited merely because it offends some listeners (*Cantwell v. Connecticut*, 310 U.S. 296 (1940)). Offense should never be a reason to limit freedom of speech. In order for speech to be prohibited, the speech must be legally found to be either obscene, an incitement to violence, or an invitation to fight. Yet offense is far too often becoming the reason that is illegitimately used to require clearing the square of religious speech.

The legal definition of obscenity requires that speech be patently offensive in such a sexually explicit manner that the average person in the community would find the speech utterly without redeeming social value. Speech that becomes an incitement to violence when the speaker's words are likely to trigger imminent violent behavior may also be prohibited. Fighting words are not merely offensive language directed to the world at large; rather, they are the speaker's invitation for an immediate brawl.

If speech is merely offensive to some listeners, it does not fall into any of the above-prohibited categories. Any prohibition of speech merely because that speech represents an unpopular viewpoint or offends the hearer cannot be constitutionally upheld. However, that standard is coming under attack as courts are beginning to grant standing to citizens who claim to be offended at hearing religious speech or prayer in public. Harassment, now often defined as any speech that is unwelcome, is also a criteria now being used to limit religious speech.

The First Amendment's guarantees of freedom of religion and speech have continued to preserve the right to witness to others in America. While the Apostles were faced with imprisonment and even execution for spreading the Gospel, thus far the Christian's right to witness has generally been constitutionally protected; however, Christians must remain vigilant and involved in the political process or they could quickly see their religious liberties eroded in a culture that is becoming less and less tolerant of public religious expression—and particularly Christianity.

Chapter 9

Other Provisions of the Bill of Rights

The Bill of Rights, as enacted, became the first
ten amendments to the Constitution.

The first ten amendments to the Constitution make up the Bill of Rights and were intended to identify important rights the new nation specifically wanted to preserve for individuals and the states themselves. The text of the Bill of Rights has remained unchanged for more than two hundred years, although, as with the various Articles of the Constitution, the interpretation of that text by the courts has changed drastically over time.

When Congress originally adopted the first set of amendments to the Constitution on September 25, 1789, there were actually 12 amendments, not 10. Two of these amendments, however, were not ratified by the states at that time. One of these two addressed the timing of congressional pay raises (this later became the Twenty-seventh Amendment, ratified in 1992), and the other would have changed the apportionment of Congress (but has never been ratified by the states). The original 12 amendments adopted by Congress were sent to each state to become ratified and become part of the Bill of Rights upon approval by 2/3 of the states. On December 15, 1791, Virginia became the last state necessary to ratify the 10 amendments that became known as the Bill of Rights. These 10 amendments stand apart as the most basic rights guaranteed under the Constitution. The following chapter presents an overview of key provisions in the Bill of Rights and a brief commentary on each amendment. (See Appendix 2 for a complete copy of all of the Constitutional Amendments, including the Bill of Rights.)

I. THE PURPOSE OF THE BILL OF RIGHTS

One fundamental purpose of the Bill of Rights was the preservation of state and individual autonomy. Many of the Founding Fathers thought the Bill of Rights was absolutely necessary for the furtherance of ordered liberty. Without the promise of the Bill of Rights, the Constitution would not have been ratified. Many of the Founders opposed the centralization of power in the federal government without sufficient safeguards for state sovereignty. A group called the "Anti-Federalists" warned at the time that unless specific amendments were added to the Constitution to limit the federal government's power, the federal government might envelop and annul the rights of individual states and citizens.

Because of the Founders' strong opposition to an all-powerful central government, the original purpose of the Bill of Rights was intended to restrict the power of the federal government, not that of the states. Samuel Adams noted that the Bill of Rights was created "*to see a line drawn as clearly as may be between the federal powers vested in Congress and the distinct sovereignty of the several States upon which the private and personal rights of the citizens depend.*"[1] This fact was recognized by the United States Supreme Court in the 1833 decision of *Barron v. Baltimore*, 32 U.S. 243 (1833), in which Chief Justice John Marshall ruled that the Bill of Rights did not apply to the individual state governments.

Following the ratification of the Fourteenth Amendment and the demise of the common law, the Supreme Court began to individually apply the provisions of the Bill of Rights to the states and to local governments rather than only to the federal government through the incorporation doctrine. The effects of incorporation on First Amendment liberties have been generally positive with respect to free speech protections, while not so positive with respect to the religion clauses (Free Exercise and Establishment clauses).

II. SPECIFIC PROVISIONS OF THE BILL OF RIGHTS

Most of the provisions of the Bill of Rights have now been incorporated through the Fourteenth Amendment to apply to states as well as to the federal government.

A. The First Amendment

The crucial amendments under the Bill of Rights start with the First Amendment's protection of religion, speech, press, and the rights of assembly and petition; the words "separation of church and state" do not appear even once in the First Amendment—or anywhere else in the Constitution.

The First Amendment is often considered the most important amendment in the Bill of Rights. The following excerpt from Virginia's Declaration of

Rights (1776) shows how it inspired the First Amendment:

> . . . *all men are equally entitled to the free exercise of religion,
> according to the dictates of conscience; and that it is the mutual
> duty of all to practise Christian forbearance, love, and charity
> toward each other.*

Virginia's Declaration also described the freedom of the press as "*one of
the great bulwarks of liberty.*" The English Bill of Rights (1689) inspired the
right of the people to assemble and petition government.

It is important to remember that constitutional protections apply only with
respect to actions of the government. The Constitution does not protect
citizens against the actions of private corporations or individuals. The
Constitution presumes that the rights of private entities will be protected
through contract provisions or specific statutes enacted by legislatures.
However, legislatures may not enact any laws that would interfere with
constitutionally protected rights as determined today by courts.

It is also important to remember that while persons are granted rights to
freedom of speech and press under the First Amendment, the Constitution
does not protect such persons from the negative consequences of their
exercise of these rights. Libel laws, for instance, apply even in an atmosphere
of free speech and press. Intimidation and harassment are still prohibited;
however, the definitions of what constitutes intimidation and harassment
are now often changed to disadvantage Christian speech.

The First Amendment applies to spoken, written, and symbolic speech, as
well as to words, pictures, or symbols. The exercise of one's constitutional
rights may not interfere with the exercise of those rights by others. For
instance, criminal laws such as those against trespass continue to apply;
therefore, the exercise of the right to peaceable assembly does not apply
on private property. All constitutional rights must be exercised in such
a manner as to not infringe or impair the legitimate rights of others.
Furthermore, such rights may not be exercised in violation of other duly
enacted constitutional laws to protect public and private property and to
keep the peace.

The right to petition the government for redress of grievances includes the
right to peaceful protest at all levels of government. It also includes the right
to circulate petitions and gather signatures to influence the government.
All rights protected under the Bill of Rights are subject to adjudication by

federal courts.

B. The Second Amendment

This amendment provides for the *"right of the people to keep and bear Arms."* While seemingly a straightforward provision, this Amendment has generated considerable controversy in modern America, particularly as "gun control" advocates have become politically active. Does the Amendment refer only to state militias, or do ordinary private citizens also have a constitutional right to keep and bear arms as individuals? This controversy is currently playing itself out primarily in the political, rather than the judicial, arena as legislatures consider various laws to restrict and regulate particular types of gun ownership. "Second Amendment societies" have been organized by citizens to oppose gun control laws that would leave citizens defenseless against their government, as well as against others who might seek to cause them harm.

C. The Third Amendment

This amendment protects the people from soldiers being quartered in their homes *"in time of peace . . . without the consent of the Owner, nor in time of war, but in a manner prescribed by law."* This fundamental protection was an important, direct outgrowth of the quartering of British troops in private homes in the American colonies both before and during the War for Independence. The English Petition of Rights (1628) also prohibited the king from engaging in this practice.

While it was a great concern to 18th century Americans at the time of the Revolution, at the present time its provisions are outdated and seemingly unnecessary. Nevertheless, at some future time these protections may again become relevant.

D. The Fourth Amendment

Under the Fourth Amendment, persons are protected against *"unreasonable searches and seizures"* of their persons and property, including homes and automobiles, as well as briefcases and travel bags—with the exception of searches determined to be "reasonable," such as those conducted at airports. Persons are guaranteed that no search warrant will be issued against them without a judicial determination of probable cause. This amendment came to the forefront in recent times with regard to personal information being collected by the National Security Administration.

Virginia's Declaration of Rights (1776) was the basis for protection against unreasonable search and seizures. Prior to the Revolutionary War, the British had used Writs of Assistance to search private homes for smuggled goods.

Today, the provisions of both the Fourth and Fifth Amendments apply primarily to criminal proceedings. This amendment has been the source of a great deal of criminal case law and has generally been interpreted to provide broad protections to persons accused of a crime. If police officers violate a person's rights during an investigation, the suspect may be set free without a trial. The amendment may also restrict what evidence can be produced in court during a criminal trial. If a court finds that evidence was gathered in violation of this amendment, barring an exception, the court will refuse to admit it as evidence against a defendant.

E. The Fifth Amendment

The protections of the Fifth Amendment are personal privileges applied to individuals. The rights to a grand jury and against double jeopardy were initiated by James Madison and recognized in New York's Declaration of Rights (1788). The right not to be compelled to give evidence against oneself came from Virginia's Declaration of Rights and was also protected in North Carolina's Declaration of Rights (1789). The right to due process of law was carried forward from the English Bill of Rights.

If a person is convicted of a capital or otherwise infamous crime for which the person may receive greater than a one-year prison sentence, there must be a *"presentment or indictment of a Grand jury, except in cases arising in the land or naval forces, or in the Militia, when in actual service in time of war or public danger."* Crimes involving the armed forces are tried in military courts, where military laws apply.

No person may be tried twice for the same offense—i.e., may not be held in double jeopardy. Nevertheless, a person may be subject to both criminal and civil action for the same offense. As seen in the trial of the famous football star O.J. Simpson, even when a person is acquitted in criminal court, he may successfully be found liable for the same actions in civil court.

No person may be forced to be a witness against himself—i.e., no self-incrimination. When persons avail themselves of this right, it is called "taking the Fifth Amendment." This amendment has also given rise to the "*Miranda* warnings"[8] made popular by TV crime shows. The name *Miranda* is derived from the case *Miranda v. Arizona*, 384 U.S. 436 (1966) in which the Supreme Court identified this constitutional protection. If this warning is not given by arresting officers, statements or confessions made by the defendant may not be admitted as evidence against him at trial, barring some type of exception or extenuating circumstance.

Fifth Amendment protections assure that no person may be deprived of life, liberty, or property without due process of law. The due process clause provides very broad protections in criminal, civil, and administrative law. Due process generally involves the requirements of notice of the charges against a person and a fair hearing. Following the passage of an additional due process section in the Fourteenth Amendment, courts have also carved out important areas of "substantive" due process rights which protect certain rights that are considered to be fundamental, such as parental rights to oversee the upbringing and education of their children. These provisions generate broad protections as defined by courts. Again, these rights are in danger of being redefined by modern governmental regulations. Citizens must be particularly concerned with protecting the right of parents to homeschool their children or to educate them in religious schools, a right that already has been undermined in Europe, where the government claims that its rights trump those of the parents with regard to educating children according to the dictates of the state.

Finally, the Fifth Amendment provides that no citizen's private property shall be taken for public use without just compensation. Laws with regard to the taking of property by the government are referred to as laws of "eminent domain." The Supreme Court, however, has been expanding the situations under which public takings are permitted. Initially, such takings were only permitted for public uses such as highways and public buildings. In 2005, however, the Court expanded this permission to include taking private property if the public use is considered to improve economic

---

[8] Pursuant to *Miranda*, "[p]rior to any questioning, the person must be warned that he has a right to remain silent, that any statement he does make may be used as evidence against him, and that he has a right to the presence of an attorney, ... The defendant may waive... these rights, provided the waiver is made voluntarily, knowingly and intelligently. If, however, he indicates in any manner and at any stage of the process that he wishes to consult with an attorney before speaking, there can be no questioning. Likewise, if the individual is alone and indicates in any manner that he does not wish to be interrogated, the police may not question him. The mere fact that he may have answered some questions or volunteered some statements on his own does not deprive him of the right to refrain from answering any further inquiries until he has consulted with an attorney and thereafter consents to be questioned." *Miranda v. Arizona*, 384 U.S. 436, 444 (1966)

opportunities for the entire community. (*Kelo v. New London*, 545 U.S. 469 (2005)). This decision was roundly criticized by Congress as well as by ordinary property holders worried about their own future. Some states and local governments have since enacted laws to prevent private property takeovers for mere economic reasons.

F. The Sixth Amendment

This amendment guarantees that, in criminal matters, the accused will be provided with a speedy public trial by an impartial jury; will have full information regarding the accusation; will be permitted to have face-to-face confrontation by the witnesses against him; will participate in a compulsory process for obtaining witnesses; and, will have effective assistance of legal counsel. These rights have been incorporated to cover state as well as federal criminal proceedings.

The right to trial by jury was drawn from the English Magna Carta (1215), Virginia's Declaration of Rights (1776), and North Carolina's Declaration of Rights (1776). Virginia's Declaration is also the source for the right of a defendant to be confronted with accusers and witnesses, to call for evidence in his favor, and to a speedy trial.

Determinations regarding the implementation of the Fourth, Fifth, and Sixth Amendments have been the subject of numerous court actions in which the rights of persons involved in various criminal actions have been expanded on a case-by-case basis. Expansions of the rights guaranteed by these amendments were especially common during the 1950s and 60s, when former governor of California, Earl Warren, served as Chief Justice of the United States Supreme Court.

G. The Seventh Amendment

The Seventh Amendment provides the basis for determining when jury trials are constitutionally required in civil (non-criminal) federal cases. It also prohibits facts from being re-tried by another jury or court at a later time. Courts have provided for specific requirements to be followed in jury selection and procedure.

H. The Eighth Amendment

This amendment provides a guarantee against "excessive bail" and "excessive fines" being imposed. It also protects against "cruel and unusual punishment" being inflicted. The English Bill of Rights and Virginia's Declaration of Rights inspired the prohibition on excessive bail and fines and cruel and unusual punishment.

The key controversies that impact modern interpretations of this amendment generally involve the limits of what punishment is considered "cruel and unusual." Some opponents of the death penalty have argued that in modern America, the death penalty itself constitutes cruel and unusual punishment even though that inclusion was clearly not part of the original intent of this amendment.

I. The Ninth Amendment

The Ninth Amendment was written to protect against the federal government threatening those common law rights belonging to the people but not specifically named in the Constitution. Today, such rights are very limited indeed, although this amendment has been one of the amendments used by courts to find an implied right to privacy in the Constitution, such as the right to privacy involved in cases of contraception, abortion, or the right to engage in sexual immorality.

J. The Tenth Amendment

Our Constitution provides for a government that is limited by delegated and specifically enumerated powers. The Tenth Amendment was intended to preserve for states and individuals those powers not specifically given to the federal government. The issue of "federalism," or which rights are reserved for the states and the people, is an ongoing concern of federal courts and constitutes a somewhat moving target from court to court and from issue to issue.

This amendment intends that the federal government should not claim powers that are not specifically granted to it by the Constitution. As we have seen, however, historically there have been very few circumstances in which courts have not found some constitutional provision or other on which to base a federal jurisdiction when the court desires to find one.

Chapter 10

Other Constitutional Amendments

In the more than two hundred years since the
Constitution and Bill of Rights were adopted, only
seventeen amendments have been ratified.

Only seventeen amendments to the Constitution have been enacted by
Congress and ratified by the states since the Bill of Rights was enacted in
1791. Only one of those amendments was later repealed. The following
commentary presents an overview of key provisions from the remaining
amendments. (See Appendix 2 for a complete copy of the Amendments
to the Constitution, which includes the Bill of Rights and the other
Amendments.)

I. THE INITIAL POST-BILL OF RIGHTS AMENDMENTS

The Constitution provides for Congress to propose amendments by either
a super-majority vote (2/3 of both chambers), or by a Constitutional
Convention called by at least 2/3 of the state legislatures. To date, all of the
proposed amendments have originated in Congress rather than through a
convention called by the states.

A. The Eleventh Amendment

The Eleventh Amendment was proposed by the Third Congress and
ratified by the states in 1798. This amendment provides for governmental
immunity from lawsuits by *"Citizens of another State, or by Citizens or
Subjects of any Foreign State."* Lawsuits may, however, be brought against
an officer of a state if the acts alleged fall outside of the scope of that
official's constitutional duties. Much litigation in recent years has been
focused on determining the parameters of when lawsuits may be brought
against individual government officials and when the government itself is
protected by this "sovereign immunity."

B. *The Twelfth Amendment*

The Twelfth Amendment, ratified in 1804, provides specific procedures for the Electoral College in voting for the offices of president and vice president. The amendment replaces Article II, section 1, clause 3 and was enacted in order to ensure that there would not be a tie in the Electoral College, as occurred in the election of 1800, which then threw the election into the House of Representatives.

II. THE POST CIVIL WAR AMENDMENTS

Following ratification of the Twelfth Amendment, there would be more than a half-century and an intervening Civil War before the Constitution was amended again.

A. *The Thirteenth Amendment (1865)*

Following the Civil War, the Thirteenth Amendment abolished slavery and involuntary servitude. Courts have held that neither hard labor as part of a criminal sentence nor conscription into the military fall under the proscriptions of this amendment.

The Thirteenth Amendment is the only amendment that limits both individual and governmental actions: therefore, individuals may not own slaves and governments may not support slavery.

B. *The Fourteenth Amendment (1868)*

The Fourteenth Amendment granted certain protections to citizens against the power of the state. The provisions of this amendment are far reaching, and have been the means used to apply many of the first ten amendments to the states through the "incorporation doctrine."

First, the Fourteenth Amendment stipulates that no state can abridge the privileges and immunities of citizens of the United States. This means that residents of one state are entitled to receive the same treatment as non-residents or members of other states. Generally, no preferential treatment can be given to in-state residents. An exception arises when a state has a substantial reason for giving its own residents preference.

Additionally, the Fourteenth Amendment decrees that no state may deprive any person of life, liberty, or property without due process of law.

Due process is comprised of two elements: notice and an opportunity to be heard. Unless a citizen receives warning that his behavior is in violation of the law, and additionally, has a chance to be heard in front of an impartial decision maker, he has been deprived of due process under the Fourteenth Amendment. Due process involves both procedural due process and substantive due process (which is the protection of rights that are considered fundamental, such as parental rights).

The Equal Protection clause of the Fourteenth Amendment prohibits any state from depriving any person in its jurisdiction of the equal protection of law. Specifically, if a law discriminates against a person because of race/ethnic origin, alienage/citizenship, gender, illegitimacy, or if the state's law impedes the exercise of a citizen's fundamental right, the state's law is subjected to a more rigorous standard of scrutiny. The burden rests on the state to show that a particular state interest warrants discriminatory treatment of its citizens. This section of the amendment simply means that the law guarantees equal treatment under the same conditions and among persons who are similarly situated.

The Fourteenth Amendment also disqualifies a person from holding any political or military office if that person has been guilty of rebellion or treason, although Congress may by a two-thirds vote remove the disqualification from an individual. Finally, this amendment justifies the validity of any public debt of the United States.

C. The Fifteenth Amendment (1870)

This amendment guarantees the right of every U.S. citizen to vote regardless of "*race, color, or previous condition of servitude.*" The provision was considered necessary after freeing the slaves in order to guarantee their voting rights as free citizens. Congress passed the first voting rights act (originally called The Enforcement Act) under this amendment in 1870. The act was broadened after the Civil Rights Movement in 1964 and again in 1965, when it was referred to as the Voting Rights Act.

III. KEY AMENDMENTS OF THE TWENTIETH CENTURY

A. The Sixteenth Amendment (1913)

The Sixteenth Amendment gave Congress the power to collect taxes based on income. This, in effect, repealed Article I, §9, cl. 4 of the Constitution that had prohibited capitation, or "per-person" taxes, as well as other direct taxes by the federal government unless such taxes were in direct proportion to the state's population. Although many have argued that the only "fair" way to tax income is through a flat tax (where everyone's income is taxed at the same percentage, such as 10 or 15%), the federal income tax system that resulted from the Sixteenth Amendment is that of a graduated income tax, where the percentage of taxes owed increases as a person's income increases.

B. The Seventeenth Amendment (1913)

This amendment, also ratified in 1913, changed the manner in which senators were elected. Under provisions of the original Constitution, senators were selected by their state legislators. This amendment provided for the direct election of senators by the people of each state. A state's executive officer (e.g., the governor) may make temporary appointments in the event of a vacancy in the office until an election is held.

Some commentators have noted that since this amendment was ratified, the federal government has grown at the expense of the states. Instead of changing senators as state legislatures change from one political party to another, U.S. senators may now remain in office as long as they are able to convince individuals to vote for them. This generally involves great financial expenditures and almost constant campaigns. Many citizens believe that direct elections have made senators less attentive to state issues than to national issues, where funds can be raised and favors can be given.

C. The Eighteenth Amendment (1919)

This amendment was repealed by the Twenty-first Amendment in 1933. Popularly known as Prohibition, it was a failed attempt to outlaw the sale of liquor in the United States. This is the only constitutional amendment to have later been repealed.

D. The Nineteenth Amendment (1920)

This amendment gave women the right to vote, popularly referred to as "women's suffrage." All American women were granted the right to vote after decades of agitation and protest, although some states had already permitted women to vote before 1920, such as Wyoming, which granted this right to women in 1869. This amendment was first introduced in Congress in 1878. Fifteen states (primarily in the West) and five territories gave women the right to vote prior to passage of this amendment.

E. The Twentieth Amendment (1933)

This amendment sets the precise date for the ending of one presidential term of office and the start of the following term. The date is fixed at noon on the third day of January in the year in which such terms would have ended. Transportation had reached a point of reliability where such a date could be fixed by law following an election. This amendment also provided for the manner of selecting the person who is to act as president when neither the president nor vice president is qualified or available. Congress has provided for a detailed order of succession to the office of President.

F. The Twenty-First Amendment (1933)

This amendment repealed the Eighteenth Amendment and Prohibition. It also provides for states and localities to continue to enact laws either prohibiting or regulating the sale of liquor within their own borders.

G. The Twenty-Second Amendment (1951)

This amendment specified that no person should serve as president more than twice. President George Washington had hoped to set a moral precedent during his time in office by serving only two terms; however, President Franklin D. Roosevelt served four terms and died in office. This is considered the anti-FDR amendment because it passed Congress on March 24, 1947, during Franklin Roosevelt's fourth term as President. It is designed to prevent the rise of future would-be Caesars. The amendment achieved President Washington's original goal of limiting the lust for power by permitting a president to serve for only two terms.

H. The Twenty-Third Amendment (1961)

This amendment provides for the District of Columbia, the seat of government, to participate in the Electoral College for the election of president and vice president. The number of electors would be equal to the number of representatives to the House of Representatives and to the Senate, acting in the same manner as those of a state, except that the number of such electors may never exceed that of the least populous state.

I. The Twenty-Fourth Amendment (1964)

This amendment prohibited the use of poll taxes to prevent citizens from voting. It followed on the heels of the civil rights movement that gained voting rights for minorities in a previously segregated South.

J. The Twenty-Fifth Amendment (1967)

This amendment adds to the succession of the vice president to the presidency under the terms of the Constitution and provides for the new president to appoint a new vice president, with the confirmation of two-thirds of the Senate. It also provides a procedure in the event of the temporary disability of the president. The vice president and the cabinet may determine that a disability has occurred, either physical or emotional, at which point the vice president becomes the acting president until the president informs the leaders of the House and Senate that the disability no longer exists and he resumes his office. This provision may be used in a very temporary manner, such as when the president undergoes anesthesia during surgery, in order to provide for continuity of the office.

K. The Twenty-Sixth Amendment (1971)

The Twenty-sixth Amendment lowered the voting age from twenty-one to eighteen, the age at which citizens at that time could be drafted for military service.

L. The Twenty-Seventh Amendment (1992)

This amendment prohibits Congress from lowering or raising its own salaries until after the next Congressional election, which occurs every 2 years. Thus, when Congress members vote to raise their salaries, they understand that they will only benefit from the raise if they are re-elected to the next term, which allows voters an intervening say in whether a particular member of Congress will ever receive the pay increase. Interestingly, this amendment was one of the two contained within the Bill of Rights that was never ratified by the states in the late 1700's. Although several states did ratify it back then, a resurgence of interest during the late 1970's and 80's created the momentum for 3/4 of the states to ratify the amendment by 1992.

IV. SOME AMENDMENTS NOT RATIFIED.

To date, while only twenty-seven amendments have been proposed by Congress and ratified by the states, thousands of other proposed amendments have failed. For example, after the Civil War, the common law was coming under attack by modern jurists looking to remove the law from its foundation in the Bible and evolve it in ways that could be used to manipulate the general society. As a result, there were several attempts to introduce amendments that would provide for the acknowledgment of God and the authority of His law in the Preamble of the Constitution, although these attempts were unsuccessful. Several other well-known amendments that have failed to achieve either Congressional approval or state ratification are discussed in the remainder of this chapter.

A. The Blaine Amendment

In 1875, President Ulysses S. Grant responded to mounting anti-Catholic political pressure by publicly vowing to "encourage free schools, and resolve that not one dollar be appropriated to support any sectarian [meaning, Catholic] schools." To implement this vow, the Speaker of the House of Representatives, James G. Blaine of Maine, who was courting the anti-Catholic vote in a bid for the presidential nomination of the Republican Party, introduced a bill into the Congress that was intended to become the Sixteenth Amendment to the U.S. Constitution.

Blaine's Amendment, as proposed, read as follows:

No state shall make any law respecting an establishment of religion, or prohibiting the free exercise thereof; and no money raised by taxation in any State for the support of public schools, or derived from any public fund therefore, nor any public lands devoted thereto, shall ever be under the control of any religious sect [meaning, Catholic religious sect]; nor shall any money so raised or lands so devoted be divided between religious sects and denominations.

Blaine's proposed amendment failed to gain the required two-thirds majority in the Senate by four votes. When this amendment failed, individual states were encouraged to put Blaine-like amendments into their state constitutions. These amendments were intended to essentially force Catholic students to attend public school in order to more fully integrate them into American culture, which at that time was primarily Protestant. These anti-Catholic amendments have had the effect of depriving religious schools of public funding. As a result, Catholics developed their own school system without the use of public money. Today, many Protestants and evangelicals have also developed their own private schools which operate without public funding.

The sectarian basis of these religious controversies was not lost on anti-Christian humanists, such as John Dewey, who by the 1920s were seeking ways to remove religion entirely from the public school arena. These humanists began to reinterpret Blaine-like provisions in state law against "sectarian" schools. Instead of interpreting "sectarian" to mean "Catholic," these humanists began a campaign to interpret "sectarian" to incorporate Protestant religions as well. Their goal was to remove religion entirely from the public schools.

By the 1960s, humanists had taken control of both the educational establishment and the courts, both being necessary to accomplish their goal of removing religion from public schools. The Blaine Amendment's "sectarian" language thus became the battle cry for humanists opposed to all religion in public schools. In the 1960s, both prayer and Bible reading, whether from the Catholic or Protestant Bible, were removed from the public schools as "sectarian" exercises that violated the new constitutional principle of "separation of church and state." Today, state Blaine Amendments are also used as a way to oppose state vouchers and/or scholarships for religious schools and homeschoolers.

B. The Equal Rights Amendment

One of the most famous amendments to fail after decades of attempting to have it ratified by the states was the Equal Rights Amendment (ERA). The Equal Rights Amendment was intended to guarantee the absolute equality of men and women under the law. It stated: *"Equality of rights under the law shall not be denied or abridged by the United States or by any state on account of sex."*

The ERA was written in 1923 by Alice Paul, the suffragist leader and founder of the National Woman's Party (NWP). She and the NWP considered the ERA to be the next necessary step after the Nineteenth Amendment (woman's suffrage) in guaranteeing "equal justice under law" to all citizens. The ERA was introduced into every session of Congress between 1923 and 1972, when it was finally passed and sent to the states for ratification.

Congress generally imposes a time limit for ratification, which is included in the proposed amendment itself. The deadline imposed for the ERA was seven years. In this case, conservative women, led by activist Phyllis Schlafly, who were opposed to the amendment because of its potential unintended negative consequences for women and for society in general, organized to defeat its passage in state legislatures. By the time the seven-year time limit had ended, only thirty-five states had ratified the amendment, three short of the thirty-eight necessary for ratification. Congress then extended the seven-year deadline for states to ratify the amendment to June 30, 1982, but even by that deadline, no other states were added to the total needed. Since that time, the amendment has been reintroduced into every session of Congress but has consistently failed to pass. The good that this amendment was intended to do for women has now been achieved through other legislative methods, such as laws requiring equal pay for equal work, and the negative consequences have been avoided. Only radical feminists continue to support passage of this amendment.

C. 21st Century Amendments

Many more constitutional amendments have been introduced into Congress during the 21st century: more than 450 during just the first decade alone! Many of these 21st century proposed amendments were attempts to check the extraordinary powers being exercised by the federal judiciary. Others focused on issues such as a balanced budget, school prayer, the Pledge of Allegiance, term limits, citizenship, and the District of Columbia.

Several proposed constitutional amendments specifically focused on moral and religious issues; however, all failed to pass the Congress. For instance, the text of one proposed amendment was a direct response to the Ninth Circuit Court of Appeals decision in *Newdow v. U.S. Congress*, 292 F.3d 597 (9th Cir. 2002), finding the recitation of the Pledge of Allegiance in public schools unconstitutional, a decision that was dismissed by the United States Supreme Court in 2004 without determining the substantive issue involved.

A school prayer amendment was proposed to override the U.S. Supreme Court's 1962's decision in *Engel v. Vitale*, 370 U.S. 421 (1962) that banned government-sponsored prayer in classrooms. That same proposed amendment was also intended to protect the Pledge of Allegiance to the Flag and display of the Ten Commandments.

V. THE PROPOSED FEDERAL MARRIAGE AMENDMENT (FMA)

In 2004, the Senate narrowly defeated a proposed amendment that would define marriage as solely between one man and one woman. That proposed amendment states:

Marriage in the United States shall consist only of the union of a man and a woman. Neither this Constitution nor the constitution of any state, shall be construed to require that marriage or the legal incidents thereof be conferred upon any union other than the union of a man and a woman.

This Family Marriage Amendment was introduced in the House and Senate by pro-family leaders in order to nullify state court decisions, such as *Goodridge v. Public Health Div.*, 798 N.E.2d (Mass. 2003), a decision by the Massachusetts state Supreme Court redefining marriage in that state. Since that time, many more states have redefined marriage either through court decisions or legislative action. The issue of marriage continues to be a difficult one. Many citizens hold to a new progressive/liberal evolving standard, while many others continue to support marriage as defined by "the law of nature and of nature's God," which was the standard when the Constitution was adopted and remained so for more than 200 years. The initial redefinition of marriage cases decided by the United States Supreme Court, *Hollingsworth v. Perry*, 133 S. Ct. 2652 (2013), and *U.S. v. Windsor* 133 S.Ct. 2675 (2013), did not succeed in resolving this difficult societal issue. At the time the Supreme Court decided these cases, 38 states had already enacted state Defense of Marriage Acts (DOMAs) and/or state constitutional amendments defining marriage as between one man and one woman. This would have been enough states to ratify a constitutional amendment. However, since this did not happen, the issue remains unresolved.

Conclusion

Time may be short. It is difficult to say just how much longer American Christians will retain the opportunity to make a real change in our culture. This book on the American Constitution was written in an attempt to inform Americans of the biblical principles that undergird the founding of this great nation and that we must continue to follow if we are to survive as a free people.

We have freedom now in America, but one day it may be lost. God has not given us, or any nation, any guarantees. Our second President, John Adams, once gave a solemn admonition that must be taken seriously in the 21st century:

> *Posterity! You will never know how much it cost the present generation to preserve your freedom! I hope you will make good use of it. If you do not, I shall repent it in Heaven that I ever took half the pains to preserve it!*[1]

What is the future of religious liberty in America? Unfortunately, all current indications point to a growing conflict between the faith of Christianity and all branches and levels of American government. There is no doubt that Christians will be in court more and more frequently as new laws increasingly challenge matters relating to the faith. Consider the following:

> *As the body of man is knit and kept together in due proportion by the sinews, so every commonwealth is kept and maintained in good order by obedience. But as the sinews are racked and stretched too much, or shrink together too much, it breeds great pain and deformity in a man's body: so if obedience is too much or too little in a commonwealth, it causes much evil and disorder. For too much makes the governors forget their vocation, and to usurp upon their subjects: too little breeds a licentious liberty, and*

makes the people to forget their duty. And so in both ways the commonwealth grows out of order, and at length comes to havoc and utter destruction.[2]

Christians will be forced to take a stand for Christ in our time as never before in American history. But as we take that stand, we must do so in the right way and with the right spirit—remembering that our ultimate purpose as Christians is to glorify God in all that we do. Christians must understand that their responsibility to government is a responsibility as unto God. That is what biblical submission to government is truly all about.

Christians in America should not despair. Our hope is in Jesus Christ, and we are merely pilgrims and sojourners in this world. Christians should be optimistic about the future because we know the One who holds the future.

Our Constitution still affords us many protections as American Christians. Without a doubt, we enjoy the greatest amount of personal freedom of any nation on earth. We can still spread the Gospel without fear of imprisonment or death, although this right continues to be under attack, particularly by those who would like nothing more than to silence all those bringing a Gospel message. We can still choose to educate our children at home or in Christian schools; however, those whose children remain in public schools must stay constantly on the alert to monitor what values they are being taught. We have not yet been forced to adopt an official state religion or non-religion; but our most basic religious freedoms are coming under increasing attack today from legislatures, courts, and anti-Christian legal and societal groups.

It has been said that the only thing necessary for evil to triumph is for good men to do nothing, but even good men cannot know what to do if they do not know the source of their liberties. God has granted this nation nearly two and a half centuries of unparalleled blessings. Today, however, we are seeing the results in our national life of turning our backs on the biblical Creator God who gave us liberty.

It is not enough for Christians to know what the Constitution says, although this is vitally important. Neither is it enough merely to champion the guaranteed, God-given rights to which we are entitled. While these actions will slow the pace of the decay that is already sweeping across America and the rest of the world, our nation must ultimately return to the only true source of her protection—the God of the Bible.

This is a serious message, because this is a serious time for America. We need to pray for one another and for revival in America. The Black Regiment, still preaching from our nation's pulpits, must rally once again to set a righteous standard and to change the hearts and minds of the people. Time may be growing short to bring our Constitution and its interpretation back to its legal roots in the Declaration of Independence and in the Bible. Let us pray for God's mercy and grace as we each work to the best of our abilities to keep America true to the Pilgrim's dream of becoming a "*shining city on a hill*" and, as President Ronald Reagan acknowledged, the "*last best hope of man on earth.*"

End Notes

Introduction

[1] Survey, First Amendment Center, *State of the First Amendment: 2013*, http://www.newseum.org/news/2013/07/state-of-the-first-amendment-2013.pdf.

[2] Survey, McCormick Tribune Freedom Museum, *Americans' Awareness of First Amendment Freedoms*, http://www.forum foreducation.org/ node/147.

[3] *Id.*

[4] John Adams wrote to Thomas Jefferson in 1813:

> The general Principles, on which the Fathers Achieved Independence, were the only Principles in which that beautiful Assembly of young Gentlemen could Unite, and these Principles only could be intended by them in their Address, or by me in my Answer. And what were these general Principles? I answer, the general Principles of Christianity, in which all those Sects were united: And the general Principles of English and American Liberty, in which all those young Men United, and which had United all Parties in America in Majorities sufficient to assert and maintain her Independence.

Letter from John Adams to Thomas Jefferson (June 28, 1813) *in* THE ADAMS-JEFFERSON LETTERS: THE COMPLETE CORRESPONDENCE BETWEEN THOMAS JEFFERSON AND ABIGAIL AND JOHN ADAMS 338–340, (Lester J. Cappon ed., 1988), *available at* http://www.constitution.org /primarysources/adams principles.html.

[5] Letter from John Adams to the Officers of the First Brigade of the Third Division of the Militia of Massachusetts (October 11, 1798), *in* 9 THE WORKS OF JOHN ADAMS—SECOND PRESIDENT OF THE UNITED STATES 228–229 (Charles F. Adams ed., 1997).

Chapter 1: America's Constitution

[1] JOHN C.H. WU, FOUNTAIN OF JUSTICE 65 (1959), *in* HERBERT C. TITUS, GOD, MAN, AND LAW: THE BIBLICAL PRINCIPLES 31–38 (1994).

[2] WU, *supra* note 1, at 31.

[3] WU, *supra* note 1, at 38.

[4] Speech before the Chamber of Commerce, Elmira, New York (May 3, 1907), *reprinted in* ADDRESSES AND PAPERS OF CHARLES EVANS HUGHES, GOVERNOR OF NEW YORK, 1906–1908 139 (1908). *See also* THE AUTOBIOGRAPHICAL NOTES OF CHARLES EVANS HUGHES 143 (David J. Danelski & Joseph S. Tulchin eds., 1973).

Chapter 2: Government was God's Idea

No endnotes in this chapter.

Chapter 3: The Declaration of Independence

[1] WILLIAM BLACKSTONE, I COMMENTARIES ON THE LAWS OF ENGLAND 38–41 (1765). The English from this quote was modernized in HERBERT C. TITUS, GOD, MAN, AND LAW: THE BIBLICAL PRINCIPLES 42–44 (1994).

[2] WILLIAM BLACKSTONE, I COMMENTARIES ON THE LAWS OF ENGLAND 126 (1765).

[3] *Id.*

[4] Algernon Sidney, *Discourses Concerning Government* III:33:406, I:2:6 (1698), *available at* http://www.liberty1.org/sidney.htm. Thomas Jefferson cited Algernon Sidney's writings as one of the sources for the "authority" of the Declaration of Independence. He endorsed Sidney's *Discourses Concerning Government* as "a *rich treasure of republican principles*" and "probably *the best elementary book of the principles of government, as founded in natural right which has ever been published in any language.*" Letter from Thomas Jefferson to John Trumbull (January

18, 1789), *in* THE PAPERS OF THOMAS JEFFERSON 14:467–68 (Julian P. Boyd ed., 1950); Letter from Thomas Jefferson to Mason Locke Weems (December 13, 1804), *in* CATALOGUE OF THE LIBRARY OF THOMAS JEFFERSON 3:13 (W. Millicent Sowbery ed., 1953).

[5] John Locke, *Chapter II: The Second Treatise of Civil Government in* OF THE STATE OF NATURE (1690), *available at* http://www.constitution.org/jl/2ndtr02.htm.

[6] WILLIAM BLACKSTONE, I COMMENTARIES ON THE LAWS OF ENGLAND 120–41 (1765).

[7] WILLIAM BLACKSTONE, I COMMENTARIES ON THE LAWS OF ENGLAND 44–57 (1765). The English from this quote was modernized in HERBERT C. TITUS, GOD, MAN, AND LAW: THE BIBLICAL PRINCIPLES 44 (1994).

[8] *Id.* at 46.

[9] *Id.* at 45-46.

[10] Algernon Sidney, *Discourses Concerning Government* I:2:6, (1698), *available at* http://www.constitution.org/as/dcg_102.htm.

[11] WILLIAM BLACKSTONE, I COMMENTARIES ON THE LAWS OF ENGLAND 38–41 (1765). The English from this quote was modernized in HERBERT C. TITUS, GOD, MAN, AND LAW: THE BIBLICAL PRINCIPLES 43 (1994).

[12] "[H]appiness turns out to be an activity of the soul in accordance with virtue." ARISTOTLE, I NICOMACHEAN ETHICS 1098a13 (350 B.C.), *available at* http://www.pursuit-of-happiness.org/history-of-happiness/aristotle/.

[13] ALGERNON SIDNEY, DISCOURSES CONCERNING GOVERNMENT III:33:406-407 (1698), *available at* http://www.liberty1.org/sidney.htm.

[14] JOHN WINTHROP, A MODEL OF CHRISTIAN CHARITY (1630), *reprinted in* THE PURITANS IN AMERICA: A NARRATIVE ANTHOLOGY 91 (Heimert & Delbanco eds., 1985).

[15] PAUL JOHNSON, A HISTORY OF THE AMERICAN PEOPLE 204 (1997).

[16] JOHN EIDSMOE, CHRISTIANITY AND THE CONSTITUTION: THE FAITH OF OUR FOUNDING FATHERS 51 (1995).

[17] JOHN GUNTHER, INSIDE U.S.A., in *Looking to its Roots*, TIME, May 25, 1987, at 27.

[18] Kenneth L. Woodward & David Gates, *How the Bible Made America*, NEWSWEEK, Dec. 27, 1982, at 44.

[19] FRANKLIN P. COLE, THEY PREACHED LIBERTY: AN ANTHOLOGY OF TIMELY QUOTATIONS FROM NEW ENGLAND MINISTERS OF THE AMERICAN REVOLUTION ON THE SUBJECT OF LIBERTY: ITS SOURCE, NATURE, OBLIGATIONS, TYPES, AND BLESSINGS (1977). Because of the color of their robes, these patriotic clergy were known as the Black Regiment.

[20] PAUL JOHNSON, A HISTORY OF THE AMERICAN PEOPLE 204–05 (1997).

Chapter 4: The Articles of Confederation

No endnotes in this chapter.

Chapter 5: The Constitutional Convention of 1787

[1] JOHN EIDSMOE, CHRISTIANITY AND THE CONSTITUTION: THE FAITH OF OUR FOUNDING FATHERS 43 (1987).

[2] THE FEDERALIST NO. 30 (Alexander Hamilton).

[3] Alexander Hamilton, in WILLIAM J. FEDERER, AMERICA'S GOD AND COUNTRY 273 (2000).

[4] Letter from George Washington to Alexander Hamilton, in CATHERINE D. BOWEN, MIRACLE AT PHILADELPHIA: THE STORY OF THE CONSTITUTIONAL CONVENTION MAY TO SEPTEMBER 1787 140 (1986).

[5] Letter from Washington to Lafayette (February 7 1788), *in The Papers of George Washington, available at* http://founders.archives.gov/documents/Washington/04-06-02-0079 (emphasis added).

[6] THE FEDERALIST NO. 37 (James Madison).

[7] Quoting George Washington from BOWEN, *supra* note 4, at 140.

[8] *Id.* at 86.

[9] *Id.*

[10] *Id.* at 127.

[11] James Madison quoted Benjamin Franklin in JAMES MADISON, NOTES OF THE DEBATES IN THE FEDERAL CONVENTION OF 1787 209–210 (1787).

[12] William J. Federer quoted Jonathan Dayton in FEDERER, *supra* note 1, at 249.

[13] William J. Federer quoted Edmund Jennings Randolph in FEDERER, *supra* note 1, at 249.

Chapter 6: The Constitution

[1] *James Madison Debates in Convention* (July 11, 1787), *available at* http://avalon.law.yale.edu/18th_century/debates_711.asp.

[2] Benjamin Franklin's *Dangers of a Salaried Bureaucracy* Speech Given During the Constitutional Convention of 1787, *available at* http://www.bartleby.com/268/8/12.html.

[3] HARRY V. JAFFA, THE AMERICAN FOUNDING AS THE BEST REGIME: THE BONDING OF CIVIL AND RELIGIOUS LIBERTY (1997).

[4] Carla Howell, *Many of the 456 Federal Agencies Reported to Exist by the Federal Government Consist of Hierarchies of Agencies Within Themselves*, CENTER FOR SMALL GOVERNMENT (2009), http://www.centerforsmallgovernment.com/small-government-news/ agencies-of-the-federal-government/. In the Fall of 2013, the federal government had 2,733,000 employees. Floyd Norris, *Bloated Government? Federal Employment at 47-Year Low*, ECONOMIX (Oct. 22, 2013, 10:32 AM), http://economix.blogs.nytimes.com/2013/10/22/ bloated-government-federal-employment-at-47-year-low/?_r=0.

[5] Feross Aboukhadijeh, *Chapter 10: Launching the New Ship of State 1789–1800*, AP U.S. HISTORY STUDY NOTES, (Nov. 17, 2012), http://www.apstudynotes.org/us-history/outlines/ch apter-10-launching-the-new-ship-of-state-1789-1800/.

[6] Letter from Thomas Jefferson to Charles Hammond (1821) *in* THE WRITINGS OF THOMAS JEFFERSON MEMORIAL EDITION ME 15:331 (1904).

[7] George Mason, *Addressing the Virginia Ratifying Convention* (June 4, 1788), *available at* http://press-pubs.uchicago.edu/founders/documents /v1ch8s37.html.

[8] James Madison, *Introduction of the Bill of Rights*, *available at* http://www.usconstitution.net/ madisonbor.html.

[9] Letter from Thomas Jefferson to James Madison (March 15, 1789), *available at* http://press-pubs.uchicago.edu/founders/print_documents/ v1ch14s49.html.

[10] JOHN ADAMS, THOUGHTS ON GOVERNMENT (1776), *available at* http://www.founding.com/library/lbody.cfm? id=139&parent=54.

[11] Ellis Sandoz, *Sermon 21*, in I *Political Sermons of the Founding Era* (1730–1788).

[12] *Id.*

[13] Letter from John Adams to the Officers of the First Brigade of the Third Division of the Militia of Massachusetts (October 11, 1798), *in* IX

THE WORKS OF JOHN ADAMS—SECOND PRESIDENT OF THE UNITED STATES 228-229 (Charles F. Adams ed., 1854).

[14] There are varying reports of President Lincoln expressing this sentiment at various times and circumstances during the Civil War. However, there is no contemporaneous evidence of this specific quotation. Whether spoken by President Lincoln or not, it reflects the proper chord for every American citizen to strike.

[15] Ronald Reagan, *The Speech* (October 27, 1964), *available at* http://www.pbs.org/wgbh/americanexperience/features/general-article/reagan-quotes/.

Chapter 7: The First Amendment Religion Clauses in the Bill of Rights

[1] Letter from John Adams to the Officers of the First Brigade of the Third Division of the Militia of Massachusetts (October 11, 1798), *in* IX THE WORKS OF JOHN ADAMS—SECOND PRESIDENT OF THE UNITED STATES 228-229 (Charles F. Adams ed. 1854).

[2] Letter of Charles Carroll of Carrollton to James McHenry (November 4, 1800), *available at* http://the-american-catholic.com/2011/07/03/charles-carroll-of-carrollton-without-morals-a-republic-cannot-subsist-any-length-of-time/.

[3] RUSSELL R. STANDISH & COLLIN D. STANDISH, STRUGGLE FOR RELIGIOUS LIBERTY BY THE BAPTISTS IN VIRGINIA Chapter 25 (1998), *available at* http://www.sundaylaw.net/books/other/standish/liberty/litb25.htm.

[4] *Sandra Rennie, Virginia's Baptist Persecution 1765-1778, in* 12 JOURNAL OF RELIGIOUS HISTORY 48, *available at* http://onlinelibrary.wiley.com/doi/10.1111/j.1467-9809.1982.tb00167.x/abstract.

In addition, Baptist persecution in Virginia is described in online sources such as The Baptist Index. *See* Bruce Gourley, *Outline of Baptist Persecution in Colonial Virginia, Bruce Gourley,* THE BAPTIST INDEX, http://www.brucegourley.com/Baptists/persecutionoutline.htm (last visited on Feb. 23, 2014). Gourley describes Baptist persecutions from contemporaneous court records, compiled by Lewis P. Little in *Imprisoned Preachers and Religious Liberty in Virginia. Id.* Actions taken against Baptists included these records: "pelted with apples and stone," "ducked and nearly drowned by 20 men," "commanded to take a dram, or be whipped," "jailed for permitting a man to pray," "meeting broken up by a mob," "arrested as a vagabond and schismatic," "pulled down and hauled about by hair," "tried to suffocate him with smoke," "tried to blow him up with gun powder," "drunken rowdies put in same cell with him," "horses ridden over his hearers at jail," "dragged off stage, kicked, and cuffed about," "shot with a shot-gun," "ruffians armed with bludgeons beat him," "severely beaten with a whip," "whipped severely by the Sheriff," and "hands slashed while preaching." *See also* RICHARD COOK, THE STORY OF THE BAPTISTS 226–27 (1884).

[5] THOMAS JEFFERSON, NOTES ON THE STATE OF VIRGINIA 157–61 (1784), *available at* http://press-pubs.uchicago.edu/founders/documents /amendI_religions40.html.

[6] John Leland, *The Rights of Conscience Inalienable, in* 2 POLITICAL SERMONS OF THE AMERICAN FOUNDING ERA: 1730–1805 (1991), *available at* http://oll.libertyfund.org/?option=com_staticxt& staticfile=show.php%3Ftitle=817&chapter=69401&layout=html&Ite mid=27.

[7] Letter from Joseph Spencer to James Madison, enclosing John Leland's 10 Objections (February 28, 1788), *available at* http://readtheconstitutionstupid.com/index.php?option=com_content& view=article&id=1870:1788-letter-of-joseph-spencer-to-james-madison-enclosing-john-leland-s-objections-ten-objections&catid=129&Itemid= 616&lang=en.

[8] Mark S. Scarberry, *John Leland and James Madison: Religious Influence on the Ratification of the Constitution and on the Proposal of the Bill of Rights,* 113 PENN ST. L. REV. 733 (2008), *available at* http://www.pennstatelawreview.org/print-issues/articles/john-leland-and-james-madison-religious-influence-on-the-ratification-of-the-constitution-and-on-the-proposal-of-the-bill-of-rights/.

[9] 1 ANNALS OF CONG. 434 (1789).

[10] The letter from the Danbury Baptist Association in the State of Connecticut, assembled October 7, 1801 states:

> To Thomas Jefferson, Esq., President of the United States of America
>
> Sir,
>
> Among the many millions in America and Europe who rejoice in your election to office, we embrace the first opportunity which we have enjoyed in our collective capacity, since your inauguration, to express our great satisfaction in your appointment to the Chief Magistracy in the United States. And though the mode of expression may be less courtly and pompous than what many others clothe their addresses with, we beg you, sir, to believe, that none is more sincere.
>
> Our sentiments are uniformly on the side of religious liberty: that Religion is at all times and places a matter between God and individuals, that no man ought to suffer in name, person, or effects on account of his religious opinions, [and] that the legitimate power of civil government extends no further than to punish the man who works ill to his neighbor. But sir, our constitution of government is not specific. Our ancient charter, together with the laws made coincident therewith, were adopted as the basis of our government at the time of our revolution. And such has been our laws and usages, and such still are, [so] that Religion is considered as the first object of Legislation, and therefore what religious privileges we enjoy (as a minor part of the State) we enjoy as favors granted, and not as inalienable rights. And these favors we receive at the expense of such degrading acknowledgments, as are inconsistent with the rights of freemen. It is not to be wondered at therefore, if those who seek after power and gain, under the pretense of government and Religion, should reproach their fellow men, [or] should reproach

their Chief Magistrate, as an enemy of religion, law, and good order, because he will not, dares not, assume the prerogative of Jehovah and make laws to govern the Kingdom of Christ.

Sir, we are sensible that the President of the United States is not the National Legislator and also sensible that the national government cannot destroy the laws of each State, but our hopes are strong that the sentiment of our beloved President, which have had such genial effect already, like the radiant beams of the sun, will shine and prevail through all these States—and all the world—until hierarchy and tyranny be destroyed from the earth. Sir, when we reflect on your past services, and see a glow of philanthropy and goodwill shining forth in a course of more than thirty years, we have reason to believe that America's God has raised you up to fill the Chair of State out of that goodwill which he bears to the millions which you preside over. May God strengthen you for the arduous task which providence and the voice of the people have called you—to sustain and support you and your Administration against all the predetermined opposition of those who wish to rise to wealth and importance on the poverty and subjection of the people.

And may the Lord preserve you safe from every evil and bring you at last to his Heavenly Kingdom through Jesus Christ our Glorious Mediator.
Signed in behalf of the Association,

Nehemiah Dodge, Ephraim Robbins, The Committee, Stephen S. Nelson

Letter from Danbury Baptist Association to Thomas Jefferson (October 7, 1801), *in* 35 THE PAPERS OF THOMAS JEFFERSON 407–09 (1801), *available at* https://jeffersonpapers.princeton.edu/selected-documents/danbury-baptist-association.

Jefferson's Reply:

Messrs. Nehemiah Dodge, Ephraim Robbins, and Stephen S. Nelson, A Committee of the Danbury Baptist Association, in the State of Connecticut.

Washington, January 1, 1802

Gentlemen,

The affectionate sentiment of esteem and approbation which you are so good as to express towards me, on behalf of the Danbury Baptist Association, give me the highest satisfaction. My duties dictate a faithful and zealous pursuit of the interests of my constituents, and in proportion as they are persuaded of my fidelity to those duties, the discharge of them becomes more and more pleasing.

Believing with you that religion is a matter which lies solely between man and his God, that he owes account to none other for his faith or his worship, that the legislative powers of government reach actions only, and not opinions, I contemplate with sovereign reverence that act of the whole American people which declared that their legislature would "make no law respecting an establishment of religion, or prohibiting the free exercise thereof," thus building a wall of separation between Church and State. Adhering to this expression of the supreme will of the nation in behalf of the rights of conscience, I shall see with sincere satisfaction the progress of those sentiments which tend to restore to man all his natural rights, convinced he has no natural right in opposition to his social duties.

I reciprocate your kind prayers for the protection and blessing of the common Father and Creator of man, and tender you for yourselves and your religious association, assurances of my high respect and esteem.

Letter from to Thomas Jefferson to the Danbury Baptist Association (Jan. 1, 1802), *in* XVI THE WRITINGS OF THOMAS JEFFERSON 281–82 (Albert E. Bergh ed., 1904).

[11] *Id.*

[12] Letter from Thomas Jefferson to Reverend Samuel Miller (January 23, 1808), *available at* http://www.churchstatelaw.com/historical materials/8_8 _7.asp.

[13] David Barton, *Church in the U.S. Capitol*, WALLBUILDERS (11/10/2005), http://www.wallbuilders.com/libissuesarticles.asp?id=90.

[14] *Treaty with the Kaskaskia Indians, 1803*, *in* II INDIAN AFFAIRS: LAWS AND TREATIES (1803), *available at* http://digital.library. okstate.edu/kappler/vol2/treaties/kas0067.htm.

[15] James Madison, *Proclamation of Day of Fasting and Prayer* (July 9, 1812), *available at* http://millercenter.org/president/speeches/detail/ 3616.

[16] John T. Noonan, THE LUSTER OF OUR COUNTY: THE AMERICAN EXPERIENCE OF RELIGIOUS FREEDOM 377 (1998).

[17] Robert E. Curran, *Chapter 5, Building a College and More*, *in* THE BICENTENNIAL HISTORY OF GEORGETOWN UNIVERSITY 1789-1889 117 (1993).

Chapter 8: First Amendment Freedom of Speech

No endnotes in this chapter.

Chapter 9: Other Provisions of the Bill of Rights

[1] Letter from Samuel Adams to Elbridge Gerry (August 22, 1789), *available at* http://www.consource.org/document/samuel-adams-to-elbridge-gerry-1789-8-22/.

Chapter 10: Other Constitutional Amendments

No endnotes in this chapter.

Conclusion

[1] Letter from John Adams to Abigail Adams (April 26, 1777), *in* TREASURY OF PRESIDENTIAL QUOTATIONS 106 (Caroline T. Harnsberger ed., (1964).

[2] JOHN PONET, *Chapter IV: In What Things, and How Far Subjects Are Bound to Obey Their Princes and Governors, in* A SHORT TREATISE ON POLITICAL POWER (1556), *available at* http://www.constitution. org/cmt/ponet/polpower.htm.

Appendix 1

The Original Constitution of the United States of America

Preamble

We the People of the United States, in Order to form a more perfect Union, establish Justice, insure domestic Tranquility, provide for the common defence, promote the general Welfare, and secure the Blessings of Liberty to ourselves and our Posterity, do ordain and establish this Constitution for the United States of America.

Article I

Section 1.

All legislative Powers herein granted shall be vested in a Congress of the United States, which shall consist of a Senate and House of Representatives.

Section 2.

The House of Representatives shall be composed of Members chosen every second Year by the People of the several States, and the Electors in each State shall have the Qualifications requisite for Electors of the most numerous Branch of the State Legislature.

No Person shall be a Representative who shall not have attained to the age of twenty five Years, and been seven Years a Citizen of the United States, and who shall not, when elected, be an Inhabitant of that State in which he shall be chosen.

Representatives and direct Taxes shall be apportioned among the several States which may be included within this Union, according to their respective Numbers, which shall be determined by adding to the whole Number of free Persons, including those bound to Service for a Term of Years, and excluding Indians not taxed, three fifths of all other Persons. The actual Enumeration shall be made within three Years after the first Meeting of the Congress of the United States, and within every subsequent Term of ten Years, in such Manner as they shall by Law direct. The Number of Representatives shall not exceed one for every thirty Thousand, but each State shall have at Least one Representative; and until such enumeration shall be made, the State of New Hampshire shall be entitled to choose three, Massachusetts eight, Rhode-Island and Providence Plantations one, Connecticut five, New-York six, New Jersey four, Pennsylvania eight, Delaware one, Maryland six, Virginia ten, North Carolina five, South Carolina five, and Georgia three.

When vacancies happen in the Representation from any State, the Executive Authority thereof shall issue Writs of Election to fill such Vacancies.

The House of Representatives shall choose their Speaker and other Officers; and shall have the sole Power of Impeachment.

Section 3.
The Senate of the United States shall be composed of two Senators from each State, chosen by the Legislature thereof, for six Years; and each Senator shall have one Vote.

Immediately after they shall be assembled in Consequence of the first Election, they shall be divided as equally as may be into three Classes. The Seats of the Senators of the first Class shall be vacated at the Expiration of the second Year, of the second Class at the Expiration of the fourth Year, and of the third Class at the Expiration of the sixth Year, so that one third may be chosen every second Year; and if Vacancies happen by Resignation, or otherwise, during the Recess of the Legislature of any State, the Executive thereof may make temporary Appointments until the next Meeting of the Legislature, which shall then fill such Vacancies.

No Person shall be a Senator who shall not have attained to the Age of thirty Years, and been nine Years a Citizen of the United States, and who shall not, when elected, be an Inhabitant of that State for which he shall be chosen.

The Vice President of the United States shall be President of the

Senate but shall have no Vote, unless they be equally divided.

The Senate shall choose their other Officers, and also a President pro tempore, in the Absence of the Vice President, or when he shall exercise the Office of President of the United States.

The Senate shall have the sole Power to try all Impeachments. When sitting for that Purpose, they shall be on Oath or Affirmation. When the President of the United States is tried the Chief Justice shall preside: And no Person shall be convicted without the Concurrence of two thirds of the Members present.

Judgment in Cases of Impeachment shall not extend further than to removal from Office, and disqualification to hold and enjoy any Office of honor, Trust or Profit under the United States: but the Party convicted shall nevertheless be liable and subject to Indictment, Trial, Judgment and Punishment, according to Law.

Section 4.
The Times, Places and Manner of holding Elections for Senators and Representatives, shall be prescribed in each State by the Legislature thereof; but the Congress may at any time by Law make or alter such Regulations, except as to the Places of choosing Senators.

The Congress shall assemble at least once in every Year, and such Meeting shall be on the first Monday in December, unless they shall by Law appoint a different Day.

Section 5.
Each House shall be the Judge of the Elections, Returns and Qualifications of its own Members, and a Majority of each shall constitute a Quorum to do Business; but a smaller Number may adjourn from day to day, and may be authorized to compel the Attendance of absent Members, in such Manner, and under such Penalties as each House may provide.

Each House may determine the Rules of its Proceedings, punish its Members for disorderly Behavior, and, with the Concurrence of two thirds, expel a Member.

Each House shall keep a Journal of its Proceedings, and from time to time publish the same, excepting such Parts as may in their

Judgment require Secrecy; and the Yeas and Nays of the Members of either House on any question shall, at the Desire of one fifth of those Present, be entered on the Journal.

Neither House, during the Session of Congress, shall, without the Consent of the other, adjourn for more than three days, nor to any other Place than that in which the two Houses shall be sitting.

Section 6.
The Senators and Representatives shall receive a Compensation for their Services, to be ascertained by Law, and paid out of the Treasury of the United States. They shall in all Cases, except Treason, Felony and Breach of the Peace, be privileged from Arrest during their Attendance at the Session of their respective Houses, and in going to and returning from the same; and for any Speech or Debate in either House, they shall not be questioned in any other Place.

No Senator or Representative shall, during the Time for which he was elected, be appointed to any civil Office under the Authority of the United States, which shall have been created, or the Emoluments whereof shall have been increased during such time; and no Person holding any Office under the United States, shall be a Member of either House during his Continuance in Office.

Section 7.
All Bills for raising Revenue shall originate in the House of Representatives; but the Senate may propose or concur with amendments as on other Bills.

Every Bill which shall have passed the House of Representatives and the Senate, shall, before it become a law, be presented to the President of the United States: If he approve he shall sign it, but if not he shall return it, with his Objections to that House in which it shall have originated, who shall enter the Objections at large on their Journal, and proceed to reconsider it. If after such Reconsideration two thirds of that House shall agree to pass the Bill, it shall be sent, together with the Objections, to the other House, by which it shall likewise be reconsidered, and if approved by two thirds of that House, it shall become a Law. But in all such Cases the Votes of both Houses shall be determined by Yeas and Nays, and the Names of the Persons voting for and against the Bill shall be entered on the Journal of each House respectively. If any Bill shall not be returned by the President within ten Days (Sundays excepted) after it shall have been presented to him, the Same shall be a Law, in like Manner as if he had signed it, unless the Congress by their Adjournment prevent its Return, in which Case it shall not be a Law.

Every Order, Resolution, or Vote to which the Concurrence of the Senate and House of Representatives may be necessary (except on a question of Adjournment) shall be presented to the President of the United States; and before the Same shall take Effect, shall be approved by him, or being disapproved by him, shall be repassed by two thirds of the Senate and House of Representatives, according to the Rules and Limitations prescribed in the Case of a Bill.

Section 8.

The Congress shall have Power To lay and collect Taxes, Duties, Imposts and Excises, to pay the Debts and provide for the common Defence and general Welfare of the United States; but all Duties, Imposts and Excises shall be uniform throughout the United States;

To borrow Money on the credit of the United States;

To regulate Commerce with foreign Nations, and among the several States, and with the Indian Tribes;

To establish an uniform Rule of Naturalization, and uniform Laws on the subject of Bankruptcies throughout the United States;

To coin Money, regulate the Value thereof, and of foreign Coin, and fix the Standard of Weights and Measures;

To provide for the Punishment of counterfeiting the Securities and current Coin of the United States;

To establish Post Offices and post Roads;

To promote the Progress of Science and useful Arts, by securing for limited Times to Authors and Inventors the exclusive Right to their respective Writings and Discoveries;

To constitute Tribunals inferior to the Supreme Court;

To define and punish Piracies and Felonies committed on the high

Seas, and Offences against the Law of Nations;

To declare War, grant Letters of Marque and Reprisal, and make Rules concerning Captures on Land and Water;

To raise and support Armies, but no Appropriation of Money to that Use shall be for a longer Term than two Years;

To provide and maintain a Navy;

To make Rules for the Government and Regulation of the land and naval Forces;

To provide for calling forth the Militia to execute the Laws of the Union, suppress Insurrections and repeal Invasions;

To provide for organizing, arming, and disciplining, the Militia, and for governing such Part of them as may be employed in the Service of the United States, reserving to the States respectively, the Appointment of the Officers, and the Authority of training the Militia according to the discipline prescribed by Congress;

To exercise exclusive Legislation in all Cases whatsoever, over such District (not exceeding ten Miles square) as may, by Cession of Particular States, and the Acceptance of Congress, become the Seat of the Government of the United States, and to exercise like Authority over all Places purchased by the Consent of the Legislature of the State in which the Same shall be, for the Erection of Forts, Magazines, Arsenals, dock-Yards and other needful Buildings; —And

To make all Laws which shall be necessary and proper for carrying into Execution the foregoing Powers and all other Powers vested by this Constitution in the Government of the United States, or in any Department or Officer thereof.

Section 9.
The Migration or Importation of such Persons as any of the States now existing shall think proper to admit, shall not be prohibited by the Congress prior to the Year one thousand eight hundred and eight, but a Tax or duty may be imposed on such Importation, not exceeding ten dollars for each Person.

The Privilege of the Writ of Habeas Corpus shall not be suspended, unless when in Cases or Rebellion or Invasion the public Safety may require it.

No Bill of Attainder or ex post facto Law shall be passed.

No Capitation, or other direct, Tax shall be laid, unless in Proportion to the Census of Enumeration herein before directed to be taken.

No Tax or Duty shall be laid on Articles exported from any State.

No Preference shall be given by any Regulation of Commerce or Revenue to the Ports of one State over those of another: nor shall Vessels bound to, or from, one State, be obliged to enter, clear, or pay Duties in another.

No Money shall be drawn from the Treasury, but in Consequence of Appropriations made by Law; and a regular Statement and Account of the Receipts and Expenditures of all public Money shall be published from time to time.

No Title of Nobility shall be granted by the United States: And no Person holding any Office of Profit or Trust under them, shall, without the Consent of the Congress, accept of any present, Emolument, Office, or Title, of any kind whatever, from any King, Prince, or foreign State.

Section 10.
No State shall enter into any Treaty, Alliance, or Confederation; grant Letters of Marque and Reprisal; coin Money; emit Bills of Credit; make any Thing but gold and silver Coin a Tender in Payment of Debts; pass any Bill of Attainder, ex post facto Law, or Law impairing the Obligation of Contracts, or grant any Title of Nobility.

No State shall, without the Consent of the Congress, lay any Imposts or Duties on Imports or Exports, except what may be absolutely necessary for executing it's inspection Laws: and the net Produce of all Duties and Imposts, laid by any State on Imports or Exports, shall be for the Use of the Treasury of the United States; and all such Laws shall be subject to the Revision and Control of the Congress.

No State shall, without the Consent of Congress, lay any Duty of

Tonnage, keep Troops, or Ships of War in time of Peace, enter into any Agreement or Compact with another State, or with a foreign Power, or engage in War, unless actually invaded, or in such imminent Danger as will not admit of delay.

Article II

Section 1.

The executive Power shall be vested in a President of the United States of America. He shall hold his Office during the Term of four Years, and, together with the Vice President, chosen for the same Term, be elected, as follows:

Each State shall appoint, in such Manner as the Legislature thereof may direct, a Number of Electors, equal to the whole Number of Senators and Representatives to which the State may be entitled in the Congress: but no Senator or Representative, or Person holding an Office of Trust or Profit under the United States, shall be appointed an Elector.

The Electors shall meet in their respective States, and vote by Ballot for two Persons, of whom one at least shall not be an Inhabitant of the same State with themselves. And they shall make a List of all the Persons voted for, and of the Number of Votes for each; which List they shall sign and certify, and transmit sealed to the Seat of the Government of the United States, directed to the President of the Senate. The President of the Senate shall, in the Presence of the Senate and House of Representatives, open all the Certificates, and the Votes shall then be counted. The Person having the greatest Number of Votes shall be the President, if such Number be a Majority of the whole Number of Electors appointed; and if there be more than one who have such Majority, and have an equal Number of Votes, then the House of Representatives shall immediately choose by Ballot one of them for President; and if no Person have a Majority, then from the five highest on the List the said House shall in like Manner choose the President. But in choosing the President, the Votes shall be taken by States, the Representation from each State having one Vote; a quorum for this Purpose shall consist of a Member or Members from two thirds of the States, and a Majority of all the States shall be necessary to a Choice. In every Case, after the Choice of the President, the Person having the greatest Number of Votes of the Electors shall be the Vice President. But if there should remain two or more who have equal Votes, the Senate shall choose from them by Ballot the Vice President.

The Congress may determine the Time of choosing the Electors, and the Day on which they shall give their Votes; which Day shall be the same throughout the United States.

No Person except a natural born Citizen, or a Citizen of the United States, at the time of the Adoption of this Constitution, shall be eligible to the Office of President; neither shall any person be eligible to that Office who shall not have attained to the Age of thirty five Years, and been fourteen Years a Resident within the United States.

In Case of the Removal of the President from Office, or of his Death, Resignation, or Inability to discharge the Powers and Duties of the said Office, the Same shall devolve on the Vice President, and the Congress may by Law provide for the Case of Removal, Death, Resignation or Inability, both of the President and Vice President, declaring what Officer shall then act as President, and such Officer shall act accordingly, until the Disability be removed, or a President shall be elected.

The President shall, at stated Times, receive for his Services, a Compensation, which shall neither be increased nor diminished during the Period for which he shall have been elected, and he shall not receive within that Period any other Emolument from the United States, or any of them.

Before he enter on the Execution of his Office, he shall take the following Oath or Affirmation:—"I do solemnly swear (or affirm) that I will faithfully execute the Office of President of the United States, and will to the best of my Ability, preserve, protect and defend the Constitution of the United States."

Section 2.
The President shall be Commander in Chief of the Army and Navy of the United States, and of the Militia of the several States, when called into the actual Service of the United States; he may require the Opinion, in writing, of the principal Officer in each of the executive Departments, upon any Subject relating to the Duties of their respective Offices, and he shall have Power to Grant Reprieves and Pardons for Offences against the United States, except in Cases

of Impeachment.

He shall have Power, by and with the Advice and Consent of the Senate, to make Treaties, provided two thirds of the Senators present concur; and he shall nominate, and by and with the Advice and Consent of the Senate, shall appoint Ambassadors, other public Ministers and Consuls, Judges of the supreme Court, and all other Officers of the United States, whose Appointments are not herein otherwise provided for, and which shall be established by Law: but the Congress may by Law vest the Appointment of such inferior Officers, as they think proper, in the President alone, in the Courts of Law, or in the Heads of Departments.

The President shall have Power to fill up all Vacancies that may happen during the Recess of the Senate, by granting Commissions which shall expire at the End of their next Session.

Section 3.
He shall from time to time give to the Congress Information of the State of the Union, and recommend to their Consideration such Measures as he shall judge necessary and expedient; he may, on extraordinary Occasions, convene both Houses, or either of them, and in Case of Disagreement between them, with Respect to the Time of Adjournment, he may adjourn them to such Time as he shall think proper; he shall receive Ambassadors and other public Ministers; he shall take Care that the Laws be faithfully executed, and shall Commission all the Officers of the United States.

Section 4.
The President, Vice President and all civil Officers of the United States, shall be removed from Office on Impeachment for, and Conviction of, Treason, Bribery, or other high Crimes and Misdemeanors.

Article III

Section 1.
The judicial Power of the United States, shall be vested in one supreme Court, and in such inferior Courts as the Congress may from time to time ordain and establish. The Judges, both of the supreme and inferior Courts, shall hold their Offices during good Behavior, and shall, at stated Times, receive for their Services, a Compensation, which shall not be diminished during their Continuance in Office.

Section 2.

The judicial Power shall extend to all Cases, in Law and Equity, arising under this Constitution, the Laws of the United States, and Treaties made, or which shall be made, under their Authority;—to all Cases affecting Ambassadors, other public Ministers and Consuls;—to all Cases of admiralty and maritime Jurisdiction;—to Controversies to which the United States shall be a Party;—to Controversies between two or more States;—between a State and Citizens of another State;—between Citizens of different States;—between Citizens of the same State claiming Lands under Grants of different States, and between a State, or the Citizens thereof, and foreign States, Citizens or Subjects.

In all Cases affecting Ambassadors, other public Ministers and Consuls, and those in which a State shall be Party, the supreme Court shall have original Jurisdiction. In all the other Cases before mentioned, the supreme Court shall have appellate Jurisdiction, both as to Law and Fact, with such Exceptions, and under such Regulations as the Congress shall make.

The Trial of all Crimes, except in Cases of Impeachment, shall be by Jury; and such Trial shall be held in the State where the said Crimes shall have been committed; but when not committed within any State, the Trial shall be at such Place or Places as the Congress may by Law have directed.

Section 3.

Treason against the United States, shall consist only in levying War against them, or in adhering to their Enemies, giving them Aid and Comfort. No Person shall be convicted of Treason unless on the Testimony of two Witnesses to the same overt Act, or on Confession in open Court.

The Congress shall have Power to declare the Punishment of Treason, but no Attainder of Treason shall work Corruption of Blood, or Forfeiture except during the Life of the Person attained.

Article IV

Section 1.

Full Faith and Credit shall be given in each State to the public Acts, Records, and judicial Proceedings of every other State. And the Congress may by general Laws prescribe the Manner in which such

Acts, Records and Proceedings shall be proved, and the Effect thereof.

Section 2.
The Citizens of each State shall be entitled to all Privileges and Immunities of Citizens in the several States.

A Person charged in any State with Treason, Felony, or other Crime, who shall flee from Justice, and be found in another State, shall on Demand of the executive Authority of the State from which he fled, be delivered up, to be removed to the State having Jurisdiction of the Crime.

No Person held to Service or Labour in one State, under the Laws thereof, escaping into another, shall, in Consequence of any Law or Regulation therein, be discharged from such Service or Labour, but shall be delivered up on Claim of the Party to whom such Service or Labour may be due.

Section 3.
New States may be admitted by the Congress into this Union; but no new State shall be formed or erected within the Jurisdiction of any other State; nor any State be formed by the Junction of two or more States, or Parts of States, without the Consent of the Legislatures of the States concerned as well as of the Congress.

The Congress shall have Power to dispose of and make all needful Rules and Regulations respecting the Territory or other Property belonging to the United States; and nothing in this Constitution shall be so construed as to Prejudice any Claims of the United States, or of any particular State.

Section 4.
The United States shall guarantee to every State in this Union a Republican Form of Government, and shall protect each of them against Invasion; and on Application of the Legislature, or of the Executive (when the Legislature cannot be convened) against domestic Violence.

Article V

The Congress, whenever two thirds of both Houses shall deem it necessary, shall propose Amendments to this Constitution, or, on the Application of the Legislatures of two thirds of the several States, shall call a Convention for proposing Amendments, which, in either Case, shall be valid to all Intents and Purposes, as Part of this Constitution, when ratified by the Legislatures of three fourths of the several States, or by Conventions in three fourths thereof, as the one or the other Mode of Ratification may be proposed by the Congress; Provided that no Amendment which may be made prior to the Year One thousand eight hundred and eight shall in any Manner affect the first and fourth Clauses in the Ninth Section of the first Article; and that no State, without its Consent, shall be deprived of its equal Suffrage in the Senate.

Article VI

All Debts contracted and Engagements entered into, before the Adoption of this Constitution, shall be as valid against the United States under this Constitution, as under the Confederation.

This Constitution, and the Laws of the United States which shall be made in Pursuance thereof; and all Treaties made, or which shall be made, under the Authority of the United States, shall be the supreme Law of the Land; and the Judges in every State shall be bound thereby, any Thing in the Constitution or Laws of any state to the Contrary notwithstanding.

The Senators and Representatives before mentioned, and the Members of the several State Legislatures, and all executive and judicial Officers, both of the United States and of the several States, shall be bound by Oath or Affirmation, to support this Constitution; but no religious Test shall ever be required as a Qualification to any Office or public Trust under the United States.

Article VII

The Ratification of the Conventions of nine States, shall be sufficient for the Establishment of this Constitution between the States so ratifying the same.

Done in Convention, by the unanimous consent of the States present, the seventeenth day of September, in the year of our Lord one thousand seven hundred and eighty-seven, and of the Independence of the United States of America the twelfth. In witness whereof, we have hereunto subscribed our names.

GEORGE WASHINGTON, President, (and Deputy from Virginia.)
New-Hampshire. John Langdon, Nicholas Gilman.
Massachusetts. Nathaniel Gorham, Rufus King.
Connecticut. William Samuel Johnson, Roger Sherman.
New York. Alexander Hamilton.
New Jersey. William Livingston, David Brearley, William Paterson, Jonathan Dayton.
Pennsylvania. Benjamin Franklin, Thomas Mifflin, Robert Morris, George Clymer, Thomas Fitzsimons, Jared Ingersoll, James Wilson, Gouverneur Morris.
Delaware. George Read, Gunning Bedford, jun. John Dickenson, Richard Bassett, Jacob Broom.
Maryland. James M'Henry, Daniel of St. Tho. Jenifer, Daniel Carrol.
Virginia. John Blair, James Madison, jun.
North Carolina. William Blount, Richard Dobbs Spaight, Hugh Williamson.
South Carolina. John Rutledge, Charles Cotesworth Pinckney, Charles Pinckney, Pierce Butler.
Georgia. William Few, Abraham Baldwin.

In Convention Monday, September 17th 1787. Present The States of New Hampshire, Massachusetts, Connecticut, Mr. Hamilton from New York, New Jersey, Pennsylvania, Delaware, Maryland, Virginia, North Carolina, South Carolina and Georgia.

Resolved,

That the preceeding Constitution be laid before the United States in Congress assembled, and that it is the Opinion of this Convention, that it should afterwards be submitted to a Convention of Delegates, chosen in each State by the People thereof, under the Recommendation of its Legislature, for their Assent and Ratification; and that each Convention assenting to, and ratifying the Same, should give Notice thereof to the United States in Congress assembled.

Resolved,

That it is the Opinion of this Convention, that as soon as the Conventions of nine States shall have ratified this Constitution, the United States in Congress assembled should fix a Day on which Electors should be appointed by the States which shall have ratified the same, and a Day on which the Electors should assemble to vote for the President, and the Time and Place for commencing Proceedings under this Constitution. That after such Publication the Electors should be appointed, and the Senators and Representatives elected: That the Electors should meet on the Day fixed for the Election of the President, and should transmit their Votes certified, signed, sealed and directed, as the Constitution requires, to the Secretary of the United States in Congress assembled, that the Senators and Representatives should convene at the Time and Place assigned; that the Senators should appoint a President of the Senate, for the sole Purpose of receiving, opening and counting the Votes for President; and, that after he shall be chosen, the Congress, together with the President, should, without Delay, proceed to execute this Constitution.

By the Unanimous Order of the Convention

Go: Washington, *President*
W. Jackson, *Secretary*

Appendix 2

The Amendments to the Constitution of the United States of America[i]

Articles in addition to, and amendment of, the Constitution of the United States of America, proposed by Congress, and ratified by the Legislatures of the several states, pursuant to the Fifth Article of the original Constitution.

Amendment I[ii]

Congress shall make no law respecting an establishment of religion, or prohibiting the free exercise thereof; or abridging the freedom of speech, or of the press; or the right of the people peaceably to assemble, and to petition the Government for a redress of grievances.

Amendment II

A well regulated Militia, being necessary to the security of a free State, the right of the people to keep and bear Arms, shall not be infringed.

Amendment III

No Soldier shall, in time of peace be quartered in any house, without the consent of the Owner, nor in time of war, but in a manner to be prescribed by law.

Amendment IV

The right of the people to be secure in their persons, houses, papers, and effects, against unreasonable searches and seizures, shall not be violated, and no Warrants shall issue, but upon probable cause, supported by Oath or affirmation, and particularly describing the place to be searched, and the persons or things to be seized.

Amendment V

No person shall be held to answer for a capital, or otherwise infamous crime, unless on a presentment or indictment of a Grand Jury, except in cases arising in the land or naval forces, or in the Militia, when in actual service in time of War or public danger; nor shall any person be subject for the same offence to be twice put in jeopardy of life or limb; nor shall be compelled in any criminal case to be a witness against himself, nor be deprived of life, liberty, or property, without due process of law; nor shall private property be taken for public use, without just compensation.

Amendment VI

In all criminal prosecutions, the accused shall enjoy the right to a speedy and public trial, by an impartial jury of the State and district wherein the crime shall have been committed, which district shall have been previously ascertained by law, and to be informed of the nature and cause of the accusation; to be confronted with the witnesses against him; to have compulsory process for obtaining witnesses in his favor, and to have the Assistance of Counsel for his defence.

Amendment VII

In Suits at common law, where the value in controversy shall exceed twenty dollars, the right of trial by jury shall be preserved, and no fact tried by a jury, shall be otherwise re-examined in any Court of the United States, than according to the rules of the common law.

Amendment VIII

Excessive bail shall not be required, nor excessive fines imposed, nor cruel and unusual punishments inflicted.

Amendment IX

The enumeration in the Constitution, of certain rights, shall not be construed to deny or disparage others retained by the people.

Amendment X

The powers not delegated to the United States by the Constitution, nor prohibited by it to the States, are reserved to the States respectively, or to the people.

Amendment XI[iii]

The Judicial power of the United States shall not be construed to extend to any suit in law or equity, commenced or prosecuted against one of the United States by Citizens of another State, or by Citizens or Subjects of any Foreign State.

Amendment XII[iv]

The Electors shall meet in their respective states and vote by ballot for President and Vice-President, one of whom, at least, shall not be an inhabitant of the same state with themselves; they shall name in their ballots the person voted for as President, and in distinct ballots the person voted for as Vice- President, and they shall make distinct lists of all persons voted for as President, and of all persons voted for as Vice-President, and of the number of votes for each, which lists they shall sign and certify, and transmit sealed to the seat of the government of the United States, directed to the President of the Senate;—The President of the Senate shall, in the presence of the Senate and House of Representatives, open all the certificates and the votes shall then be counted;—The person having the greatest Number of votes for President, shall be the President, if such number be a majority of the whole number of Electors appointed; and if no person have such majority, then from the persons having the highest numbers not exceeding three on the list of those voted for as President, the House of Representatives shall choose immediately, by ballot, the President. But in choosing the President, the votes shall be taken by states, the representation from each state having one vote; a quorum for this purpose shall consist of a member or members from two-thirds of the states, and a majority of all the states shall be necessary to a choice. And if the House of Representatives shall not choose a President whenever the right of choice shall devolve upon them, before the fourth day of March next following, then the Vice- President shall act as President, as in the case of the death or other constitutional disability of the President—The person having the greatest number of votes as Vice-President, shall be the Vice-President, if such number be a majority of the whole number of Electors appointed, and if no person have a majority, then from the two highest numbers on the list, the Senate shall choose the Vice-President; a quorum for the purpose shall consist of two-thirds of the whole number of Senators, and a majority of the whole number shall be necessary to a choice. But no person constitutionally ineligible to the office of President shall be eligible to that of Vice-President of the United States.

Amendment XIII[v]

Section 1.
Neither slavery nor involuntary servitude, except as a punishment for crime whereof the party shall have been duly convicted, shall exist within the United States, or any place subject to their jurisdiction.

Section 2.
Congress shall have power to enforce this article by appropriate legislation.

Amendment XIV[vi]

Section. 1.
All persons born or naturalized in the United States and subject to the jurisdiction thereof, are citizens of the United States and of the State wherein they reside. No State shall make or enforce any law which shall abridge the privileges or immunities of citizens of the United States; nor shall any State deprive any person of life, liberty, or property, without due process of law; nor deny to any person within its jurisdiction the equal protection of the laws.

Section. 2.
Representatives shall be apportioned among the several States according to their respective numbers, counting the whole number of persons in each State, excluding Indians not taxed. But when the right to vote at any election for the choice of electors for President and Vice President of the United States, Representatives in Congress, the Executive and Judicial officers of a State, or the members of the Legislature thereof, is denied to any of the male inhabitants of such State, being twenty-one years of age, and citizens of the United States, or in any way abridged, except for participation in rebellion, or other crime, the basis of representation therein shall be reduced in the proportion which the number of such male citizens shall bear to the whole number of male citizens twenty-one years of age in such State.

Section. 3.
No person shall be a Senator or Representative in Congress, or elector of President and Vice President, or hold any office, civil or military,

under the United States, or under any State, who, having previously taken an oath, as a member of Congress, or as an officer of the United States, or as a member of any State legislature, or as an executive or judicial officer of any State, to support the Constitution of the United States, shall have engaged in insurrection or rebellion against the same, or given aid or comfort to the enemies thereof. But Congress may by a vote of two-thirds of each House, remove such disability.

Section. 4.
The validity of the public debt of the United States, authorized by law, including debts incurred for payment of pensions and bounties for services in suppressing insurrection or rebellion, shall not be questioned. But neither the United States nor any State shall assume or pay any debt or obligation incurred in aid of insurrection or rebellion against the United States, or any claim for the loss or emancipation of any slave; but all such debts, obligations and claims shall be held illegal and void.

Section. 5.
The Congress shall have power to enforce, by appropriate legislation, the provisions of this article.

Amendment XV[vii]

Section. 1.
The right of citizens of the United States to vote shall not be denied or abridged by the United States or by any State on account of race, color, or previous condition of servitude.

Section. 2.
The Congress shall have power to enforce this article by appropriate legislation.

Amendment XVI[viii]

The Congress shall have power to lay and collect taxes on incomes, from whatever source derived, without apportionment among the several States, and without regard to any census or enumeration.

Amendment XVII[ix]

The Senate of the United States shall be composed of two Senators from each State, elected by the people thereof, for six years; and each Senator shall have one vote. The electors in each State shall have the qualifications requisite for electors of the most numerous branch of the State legislatures.

When vacancies happen in the representation of any State in the Senate, the executive authority of such State shall issue writs of election to fill such vacancies: Provided, That the legislature of any State may empower the executive thereof to make temporary appointments until the people fill the vacancies by election as the legislature may direct.

This amendment shall not be so construed as to affect the election or term of any Senator chosen before it becomes valid as part of the Constitution.

Amendment XVIII[x]

Section. 1.
After one year from the ratification of this article the manufacture, sale, or transportation of intoxicating liquors within, the importation thereof into, or the exportation thereof from the United States and all territory subject to the jurisdiction thereof for beverage purposes is hereby prohibited.

Section 2.
The Congress and the several States shall have concurrent power to enforce this article by appropriate legislation.

Section 3.
This article shall be inoperative unless it shall have been ratified as an amendment to the Constitution by the legislatures of the several States, as provided in the Constitution, within seven years from the date of the submission hereof to the States by the Congress.

Amendment XIX[xi]

The right of citizens of the United States to vote shall not be denied or abridged by the United States or by any State on account of sex. Congress shall have power to enforce this article by appropriate legislation.

Amendment XX[xii]

Section. 1.
The terms of the President and Vice President shall end at noon on the 20th day of January, and the terms of Senators and Representatives at noon on the 3d day of January, of the years in which such terms would have ended if this article had not been ratified; and the terms of their successors shall then begin.

Section 2.
The Congress shall assemble at least once in every year, and such meeting shall begin at noon on the 3d day of January, unless they shall by law appoint a different day.

Section 3.
If, at the time fixed for the beginning of the term of the President, the President elect shall have died, the Vice President elect shall become President. If a President shall not have been chosen before the time fixed for the beginning of his term, or if the President elect shall have failed to qualify, then the Vice President elect shall act as President until a President shall have qualified; and the Congress may by law provide for the case wherein neither a President elect nor a Vice President elect shall have qualified, declaring who shall then act as President, or the manner in which one who is to act shall be selected, and such person shall act accordingly until a President or Vice President shall have qualified.

Section 4.
The Congress may by law provide for the case of the death of any of the persons from whom the House of Representatives may choose a President whenever the right of choice shall have devolved upon them, and for the case of the death of any of the persons from whom the Senate may choose a Vice President whenever the right of choice shall have devolved upon them.

Section 5.
Sections 1 and 2 shall take effect on the 15th day of October following the ratification of this article.

Section 6.
This article shall be inoperative unless it shall have been ratified as an amendment to the Constitution by the legislatures of three-fourths of

the several States within seven years from the date of its submission.

Amendment XXI[xiii]

Section. 1.
The eighteenth article of amendment to the Constitution of the United States is hereby repealed.

Section 2.
The transportation or importation into any State, Territory, or possession of the United States for delivery or use therein of intoxicating liquors, in violation of the laws thereof, is hereby prohibited.

Section 3.
This article shall be inoperative unless it shall have been ratified as an amendment to the Constitution by conventions in the several States, as provided in the Constitution, within seven years from the date of the submission hereof to the States by the Congress.

Amendment XXII[xiv]

Section. 1.
No person shall be elected to the office of the President more than twice, and no person who has held the office of President, or acted as President, for more than two years of a term to which some other person was elected President shall be elected to the office of the President more than once. But this Article shall not apply to any person holding the office of President, when this Article was proposed by the Congress, and shall not prevent any person who may be holding the office of President, or acting as President, during the term within which this Article becomes operative from holding the office of President or acting as President during the remainder of such term.

Section 2.
This article shall be inoperative unless it shall have been ratified as an amendment to the Constitution by the legislatures of three-fourths of the several States within seven years from the date of its submission to the States by the Congress.

Amendment XXIII[xv]

Section. 1.
The District constituting the seat of Government of the United States shall appoint in such manner as the Congress may direct: A number of electors of President and Vice President equal to the whole number of Senators and Representatives in Congress to which the District would be entitled if it were a State, but in no event more than the least populous State; they shall be in addition to those appointed by the States, but they shall be considered, for the purposes of the election of President and Vice President, to be electors appointed by a State; and they shall meet in the District and perform such duties as provided by the twelfth article of amendment.

Section 2.
The Congress shall have power to enforce this article by appropriate legislation.

Amendment XXIV[xvi]

Section. 1.
The right of citizens of the United States to vote in any primary or other election for President or Vice President, for electors for President or Vice President, or for Senator or Representative in Congress, shall not be denied or abridged by the United States or any State by reason of failure to pay any poll tax or other tax.

Section. 2.
The Congress shall have power to enforce this article by appropriate legislation.

Amendment XXV[xvii]

Section. 1.
In case of the removal of the President from office or of his death or resignation, the Vice President shall become President.

Section. 2.
Whenever there is a vacancy in the office of the Vice President, the President shall nominate a Vice President who shall take office upon confirmation by a majority vote of both Houses of Congress.

Section. 3.
Whenever the President transmits to the President pro tempore of the Senate and the Speaker of the House of Representatives his written declaration that he is unable to discharge the powers and duties of his office, and until he transmits to them a written declaration to the contrary, such powers and duties shall be discharged by the Vice President as Acting President.

Section. 4.
Whenever the Vice President and a majority of either the principal officers of the executive departments or of such other body as Congress may by law provide, transmit to the President pro tempore of the Senate and the Speaker of the House of Representatives their written declaration that the President is unable to discharge the powers and duties of his office, the Vice President shall immediately assume the powers and duties of the office as Acting President.

Thereafter, when the President transmits to the President pro tempore of the Senate and the Speaker of the House of Representatives his written declaration that no inability exists, he shall resume the powers and duties of his office unless the Vice President and a majority of either the principal officers of the executive department or of such other body as Congress may by law provide, transmit within four days to the President pro tempore of the Senate and the Speaker of the House of Representatives their written declaration that the President is unable to discharge the powers and duties of his office. Thereupon Congress shall decide the issue, assembling within forty-eight hours for that purpose if not in session. If the Congress, within twenty-one days after receipt of the latter written declaration, or, if Congress is not in session, within twenty-one days after Congress is required to assemble, determines by two-thirds vote of both Houses that the President is unable to discharge the powers and duties of his office, the Vice President shall continue to discharge the same as Acting President; otherwise, the President shall resume the powers and duties of his office.

Amendment XXVI[xviii]

Section. 1.
The right of citizens of the United States, who are eighteen years of age or older, to vote shall not be denied or abridged by the United

States or by any State on account of age.

Section. 2.
The Congress shall have power to enforce this article by appropriate legislation.

Amendment XXVII[xix]

No law varying the compensation for the services of the Senators and Representatives shall take effect, until an election of Representatives shall have intervened.

Endnotes to Appendix 2

These endnotes are provided by the United States Senate from the United States Government Printing Office. No copyright claim is made with respect to original U.S. Government works. Retrieved from http://www.gpo.gov/fdsys/pkg/GPO-CONAN-1992/pdf/GPO-CONAN-1992-7.pdf

[i] In *Dillon v. Gloss*, 256 U.S. 368 (1921), the Supreme Court stated that it would take judicial notice of the date on which a State ratified a proposed constitutional amendment. Accordingly the Court consulted the State journals to determine the dates on which each house of the legislature of certain States ratified the Eighteenth Amendment. It, therefore, follows that the date on which the governor approved the ratification, or the date on which the secretary of state of a given State certified the ratification, or the date on which the Secretary of State of the United States received a copy of said certificate, or the date on which he proclaimed that the amendment had been ratified are not controlling. Hence, the ratification date given in the following notes is the date on which the legislature of a given State approved the particular amendment (signature by the speaker or presiding officers of both houses being considered a part of the ratification of the "legislature"). When that date is not available, the date given is that on which it was approved by the governor or certified by the secretary of state of the particular State. In each case such fact has been noted. Except as otherwise indicated information as to ratification is based on data supplied by the Department of State.

[ii] Brackets enclosing an amendment number indicate that the number was not specifically assigned in the resolution proposing the amendment. It will be seen, accordingly, that only the Thirteenth, Fourteenth, Fifteenth, and Sixteenth Amendments were thus technically ratified by number. The first ten amendments along with two others that were not ratified were proposed by Congress on September 25, 1789, when they passed the Senate, having previously passed the House on September 24 (1 Annals of Congress 88, 913). They appear officially in 1 Stat. 97. Ratification was completed on December 15, 1791, when the eleventh State (Virginia) approved these amendments, there being then 14 States in the Union.

The several state legislatures ratified the first ten amendments to the Constitution on the following dates: New Jersey, November 20, 1789; Maryland, December 19, 1789; North Carolina, December 22, 1789; South Carolina, January 19, 1790; New Hampshire, January 25, 1790; Delaware, January 28, 1790; New York, February 27, 1790; Pennsylvania, March 10, 1790; Rhode Island, June 7, 1790; Vermont, November 3, 1791; Virginia, December 15, 1791. The two amendments that then failed of ratification prescribed the ratio of representation to population in the House, and specified that no law varying the compensation of members of Congress should be effective until after an intervening election of Representatives. The first was ratified by ten States (one short of the requisite number) and the second, by six States; subsequently, this second proposal was taken up by the States in the period 1980-1992 and was proclaimed as ratified as of May 7, 1992. Connecticut, Georgia, and Massachusetts ratified the first ten amendments in 1939.

[iii] The Eleventh Amendment was proposed by Congress on March 4, 1794, when it passed the House, 4 Annals of Congress 477, 478, having previously passed the Senate on January 14, Id., 30, 31. It appears officially in 1 Stat. 402. Ratification was completed on February 7, 1795, when the twelfth State (North Carolina) approved the amendment, there being then 15 States in the Union. Official announcement of ratification was not made until January 8, 1798, when President John Adams in a message to Congress stated that the Eleventh Amendment had been adopted by three-fourths of the States and that it "may now be deemed to be a part of the Constitution." In the interim South Carolina had ratified, and Tennessee had been admitted into the Union as the sixteenth State.

The several state legislatures ratified the Eleventh Amendment on the following dates: New York, March 27, 1794; Rhode Island, March 31, 1794; Connecticut, May 8, 1794; New Hampshire, June 16, 1794; Massachusetts, June 26, 1794; Vermont, between October 9 and November 9, 1794; Virginia, November 18, 1794; Georgia, November 29, 1794; Kentucky, December 7, 1794; Maryland, December 26, 1794; Delaware, January 23, 1795; North Carolina, February 7, 1795; South Carolina, December 4,

1797.

ⁱᵛ The Twelfth Amendment was proposed by Congress on December 9, 1803, when it passed the House, 13 Annals of Congress 775, 776, having previously passed the Senate on December 2. Id., 209. It was not signed by the presiding officers of the House and Senate until December 12. It appears officially in 2 Stat. 306. Ratification was probably completed on June 15, 1804, when the legislature of the thirteenth State (New Hampshire) approved the amendment, there being then 17 States in the Union. The Governor of New Hampshire, however, vetoed this act of the legislature on June 20, and the act failed to pass again by two- thirds vote then required by the state constitution. Inasmuch as Article V of the Federal Constitution specifies that amendments shall become effective "when ratified by legislatures of three-fourths of the several States or by conventions in three-fourths thereof," it has been generally believed that an approval or veto by a governor is without significance. If the ratification by New Hampshire be deemed ineffective, then the amendment became operative by Tennessee's ratification on July 27, 1804. On September 25, 1804, in a circular letter to the Governors of the several States, Secretary of State Madison declared the amendment ratified by three-fourths of the States.

The several state legislatures ratified the Twelfth Amendment on the following dates: North Carolina, December 22, 1803; Maryland, December 24, 1803; Kentucky, December 27, 1803; Ohio, between December 5 and December 30, 1803; Virginia, between December 20, 1803 and February 3, 1804; Pennsylvania, January 5, 1804; Vermont, January 30, 1804; New York, February 10, 1804; New Jersey, February 22, 1804; Rhode Island, between February 27 and March 12, 1804; South Carolina, May 15, 1804; Georgia, May 19, 1804; New Hampshire, June 15, 1804; and Tennessee, July 27, 1804. The amendment was rejected by Delaware on January 18, 1804, and by Connecticut at its session begun May 10, 1804. Massachusetts ratified this amendment in 1961.

ᵛ The Thirteenth Amendment was proposed by Congress on January 31, 1865, when it passed the House, Cong. Globe (38th Cong., 2d Sess.) 531, having previously passed the Senate on April 8, 1964. Id. (38th cong., 1st Sess.), 1940. It appears officially in 13 Stat. 567 under the date of February 1, 1865. Ratification was completed on December 6, 1865, when the legislature of the twenty-seventh State (Georgia) approved the amendment, there being then 36 States in the Union. On December 18, 1865, Secretary of State Seward certified that the Thirteenth Amendment had become a part of the Constitution, 13 Stat. 774.

The several state legislatures ratified the Thirteenth Amendment on the following dates: Illinois, February 1, 1865; Rhode Island, February 2, 1865; Michigan, February 2, 1865; Maryland, February 3, 1865; New York, February 3, 1865; West Virginia, February 3, 1865; Missouri, February 6, 1865; Maine, February 7, 1865; Kansas, February 7, 1865; Massachusetts, February 7, 1865; Pennsylvania, February 8, 1865; Virginia, February 9, 1865; Ohio, February 10, 1865; Louisiana, February 15 or 16, 1865; Indiana, February 16, 1865; Nevada, February 16, 1865; Minnesota, February 23, 1865; Wisconsin, February 24, 1865; Vermont, March 9, 1865 (date on which it was "approved" by Governor); Tennessee, April 7, 1865; Arkansas, April 14, 1865; Connecticut, May 4, 1865; New Hampshire, June 30, 1865; South Carolina, November 13, 1865; Alabama, December 2, 1865 (date on which it was "approved" by Provisional Governor); North Carolina, December 4, 1865; Georgia, December 6, 1865; Oregon, December 11, 1865; California, December 15, 1865; Florida, December 28, 1865 (Florida again ratified this amendment on June 9, 1868, upon its adoption of a new constitution); Iowa, January 17, 1866; New Jersey, January 23, 1866 (after having rejected the amendment on March 16, 1865); Texas, February 17, 1870; Delaware, February 12, 1901 (after having rejected the amendment on February 8, 1865). The amendment was rejected by Kentucky on February 24, 1865, and by Mississippi on December 2, 1865.

ᵛⁱ The Fourteenth Amendment was proposed by Congress on June 13, 1866, when it passed the House, Cong. Globe (39th Cong., 1st Sess.) 3148, 3149, having previously passed the Senate on June 8. Id., 3042. It appears officially in 14 Stat. 358 under date of June 16, 1866. Ratification was probably completed on July 9, 1868, when the legislature of the twenty-eighth State (South Carolina or Louisiana) approved the amendment, there being then 37 States in the Union. However, Ohio and New Jersey had prior to that date "withdrawn" their earlier assent to this amendment. Accordingly, Secretary of State Seward on July 20, 1868, certified that the amendment had become a part of the Constitution if the said withdrawals were ineffective. 15 Stat. 706-707. Congress on July 21, 1868, passed a joint resolution declaring the amendment a part of the Constitution and directing the Secretary to promulgate it as such. On July 28, 1868, Secretary Seward certified without reservation that the amendment was a part

of the Constitution. In the interim, two other States, Alabama on July 13 and Georgia on July 21, 1868, had added their ratifications.

The several state legislatures ratified the Fourteenth Amendment on the following dates: Connecticut, June 30, 1866; New Hampshire, July 7, 1866; Tennessee, July 19, 1866; New Jersey, September 11, 1866 (the New Jersey Legislature on February 20, 1868 "withdrew" its consent to the ratification; the Governor vetoed that bill on March 5, 1868; and it was repassed over his veto on March 24, 1868); Oregon, September 19, 1866 (Oregon "withdrew" its consent on October 15, 1868); Vermont, October 30, 1866; New York, January 10, 1867; Ohio, January 11, 1867 (Ohio "withdrew" its consent on January 15, 1868); Illinois, January 15, 1867; West Virginia, January 16, 1867; Michigan, January 16, 1867; Kansas, January 17, 1867; Minnesota, January 17, 1867; Maine, January 19, 1867; Nevada, January 22, 1867; Indiana, January 23, 1867; Missouri, January 26, 1867 (date on which it was certified by the Missouri secretary of state); Rhode Island, February 7, 1867; Pennsylvania, February 12, 1867; Wisconsin, February 13, 1867 (actually passed February 7, but not signed by legislative officers until February 13); Massachusetts, March 20, 1867; Nebraska, June 15, 1867; Iowa, March 9, 1868; Arkansas, April 6, 1868; Florida, June 9, 1868; North Carolina, July 2, 1868 (after having rejected the amendment on December 13, 1866); Louisiana, July 9, 1868 (after having rejected the amendment on February 6, 1867); South Carolina, July 8, 1868 (after having rejected the amendment on December 20, 1866); Alabama, July 13, 1868 (date on which it was "approved" by the Governor); Georgia, July 21, 1868 (after having rejected the amendment on November 9, 1866—Georgia ratified again on February 2, 1870); Virginia, October 8, 1869 (after having rejected the amendment on January 9, 1867); Mississippi, January 17, 1870; Texas, February 18, 1870 (after having rejected the amendment on October 27, 1866); Delaware, February 12, 1901 (after having rejected the amendment on February 7, 1867). The amendment was rejected (and not subsequently ratified) by Kentucky on January 8, 1867. Maryland and California ratified this amendment in 1959.

vii The Fifteenth Amendment was proposed by Congress on February 26, 1869, when it passed the Senate, Cong. Globe (40th Cong., 3rd Sess.) 1641, having previously passed the House on February 25. Id., 1563, 1564. It appears officially in 15 Stat. 346 under the date of February 27, 1869. Ratification was probably completed on February 3, 1870, when the legislature of the twenty-eighth State (Iowa) approved the amendment, there being then 37 States in the Union. However, New York had prior to that date "withdrawn" its earlier assent to this amendment. Even if this withdrawal were effective, Nebraska's ratification on February 17, 1870, authorized Secretary of State Fish's certification of March 30, 1870, that the Fifteenth Amendment had become a part of the Constitution. 16 Stat. 1131.

The several state legislatures ratified the Fifteenth Amendment on the following dates: Nevada, March 1, 1869; West Virginia, March 3, 1869; North Carolina, March 5, 1869; Louisiana, March 5, 1869 (date on which it was "approved" by the Governor); Illinois, March 5, 1869; Michigan, March 5, 1869; Wisconsin, March 5, 1869; Maine, March 11, 1869; Massachusetts, March 12, 1869; South Carolina, March 15, 1869; Arkansas, March 15, 1869; Pennsylvania, March 25, 1869; New York, April 14, 1869 (New York "withdrew" its consent to the ratification on January 5, 1870); Indiana, May 14, 1869; Connecticut, May 19, 1869; Florida, June 14, 1869; New Hampshire, July 1, 1869; Virginia, October 8, 1869; Vermont, October 20, 1869; Alabama, November 16, 1869; Missouri, January 7, 1870 (Missouri had ratified the first section of the 15th Amendment on March 1, 1869; it failed to include in its ratification the second section of the amendment); Minnesota, January 13, 1870; Mississippi, January 17, 1870; Rhode Island, January 18, 1870; Kansas, January 19, 1870 (Kansas had by a defectively worded resolution previously ratified this amendment on February 27, 1869); Ohio, January 27, 1870 (after having rejected the amendment on May 4, 1869); Georgia, February 2, 1870; Iowa, February 3, 1870; Nebraska, February 17, 1870; Texas, February 18, 1870; New Jersey, February 15, 1871 (after having rejected the amendment on February 7, 1870); Delaware, February 12, 1901 (date on which approved by Governor; Delaware had previously rejected the amendment on March 18, 1869). The amendment was rejected (and not subsequently ratified) by Kentucky, Maryland, and Tennessee. California ratified this amendment in 1962 and Oregon in 1959.

viii The Sixteenth Amendment was proposed by Congress on July 12, 1909, when it passed the House, 44 Cong. Rec. (61st Cong., 1st Sess.) 4390, 4440, 4441, having previously passed the Senate on July 5. Id., 4121. It appears officially in 36 Stat. 184. Ratification was completed on February 3, 1913, when the legislature of the thirty-sixth State (Delaware, Wyoming, or New Mexico) approved the amendment, there being then 48 States in the Union. On February 25, 1913, Secretary of State Knox certified that this amendment had become a part of the Constitution. 37 Stat. 1785.

The several state legislatures ratified the Sixteenth Amendment on the following dates: Alabama, August 10, 1909; Kentucky, February 8, 1910; South Carolina, February 19, 1910; Illinois, March 1, 1910; Mississippi, March 7, 1910; Oklahoma, March 10, 1910; Maryland, April 8, 1910; Georgia, August 3, 1910; Texas, August 16, 1910; Ohio, January 19, 1911; Idaho, January 20, 1911; Oregon, January 23, 1911; Washington, January 26, 1911; Montana, January 27, 1911; Indiana, January 30, 1911; California, January 31, 1911; Nevada, January 31, 1911; South Dakota, February 1, 1911; Nebraska, February 9, 1911; North Carolina, February 11, 1911; Colorado, February 15, 1911; North Dakota, February 17, 1911; Michigan, February 23, 1911; Iowa, February 24, 1911; Kansas, March 2, 1911; Missouri, March 16, 1911; Maine, March 31, 1911; Tennessee, April 7, 1911; Arkansas, April 22, 1911 (after having rejected the amendment at the session begun January 9, 1911); Wisconsin, May 16, 1911; New York, July 12, 1911; Arizona, April 3, 1912; Minnesota, June 11, 1912; Louisiana, June 28, 1912; West Virginia, January 31, 1913; Delaware, February 3, 1913; Wyoming, February 3, 1913; New Mexico, February 3, 1913; New Jersey, February 4, 1913; Vermont, February 19, 1913; Massachusetts, March 4, 1913; New Hampshire, March 7, 1913 (after having rejected the amendment on March 2, 1911). The amendment was rejected (and not subsequently ratified) by Connecticut, Rhode Island, and Utah.

[ix] The Seventeenth Amendment was proposed by Congress on May 13, 1912, when it passed the House, 48 Cong. Rec. (62d Cong., 2d Sess.) 6367, having previously passed the Senate on June 12, 1911. 47 Cong. Rec. (62d Cong., 1st Sess.) 1925. It appears officially in 37 Stat. 646. Ratification was completed on April 8, 1913, when the thirty-sixth State (Connecticut) approved the amendment, there being then 48 States in the Union. On May 31, 1913, Secretary of State Bryan certified that it had become a part of the Constitution. 38 Stat 2049.

The several state legislatures ratified the Seventeenth Amendment on the following dates: Massachusetts, May 22, 1912; Arizona, June 3, 1912; Minnesota, June 10, 1912; New York, January 15, 1913; Kansas, January 17, 1913; Oregon, January 23, 1913; North Carolina, January 25, 1913; California, January 28, 1913; Michigan, January 28, 1913; Iowa, January 30, 1913; Montana, January 30, 1913; Idaho, January 31, 1913; West Virginia, February 4, 1913; Colorado, February 5, 1913; Nevada, February 6, 1913; Texas, February 7, 1913; Washington, February 7, 1913; Wyoming, February 8, 1913; Arkansas, February 11, 1913; Illinois, February 13, 1913; North Dakota, February 14, 1913; Wisconsin, February 18, 1913; Indiana, February 19, 1913; New Hampshire, February 19, 1913; Vermont, February 19, 1913; South Dakota, February 19, 1913; Maine, February 20, 1913; Oklahoma, February 24, 1913; Ohio, February 25, 1913; Missouri, March 7, 1913; New Mexico, March 13, 1913; Nebraska, March 14, 1913; New Jersey, March 17, 1913; Tennessee, April 1, 1913; Pennsylvania, April 2, 1913; Connecticut, April 8, 1913; Louisiana, June 5, 1914. The amendment was rejected by Utah on February 26, 1913.

[x] The Eighteenth Amendment was proposed by Congress on December 18, 1917, when it passed the Senate, Cong. Rec. (65th Cong. 2d Sess.) 478, having previously passed the House on December 17. Id., 470. It appears officially in 40 Stat. 1059. Ratification was completed on January 16, 1919, when the thirty-sixth State approved the amendment, there being then 48 States in the Union. On January 29, 1919, Acting Secretary of State Polk certified that this amendment had been adopted by the requisite number of States. 40 Stat. 1941. By its terms this amendment did not become effective until 1 year after ratification.

The several state legislatures ratified the Eighteenth Amendment on the following dates: Mississippi, January 8, 1918; Virginia, January 11, 1918; Kentucky, January 14, 1918; North Dakota, January 28, 1918 (date on which approved by Governor); South Carolina, January 29, 1918; Maryland, February 13, 1918; Montana, February 19, 1918; Texas, March 4, 1918; Delaware, March 18, 1918; South Dakota, March 20, 1918; Massachusetts, April 2, 1918; Arizona, May 24, 1918; Georgia, June 26, 1918; Louisiana, August 9, 1918 (date on which approved by Governor); Florida, November 27, 1918; Michigan, January 2, 1919; Ohio, January 7, 1919; Oklahoma, January 7, 1919; Idaho, January 8, 1919; Maine, January 8, 1919; West Virginia, January 9, 1919; California, January 13, 1919; Tennessee, January 13, 1919; Washington, January 13, 1919; Arkansas, January 14, 1919; Kansas, January 14, 1919; Illinois, January 14, 1919; Indiana, January 14, 1919; Alabama, January 15, 1919; Colorado, January 15, 1919; Iowa, January 15, 1919; New Hampshire, January 15, 1919; Oregon, January 15, 1919; Nebraska, January 16, 1919; North Carolina, January 16, 1919; Utah, January 16, 1919; Missouri, January 16, 1919; Wyoming, January 16, 1919; Minnesota, January 17, 1919; Wisconsin, January 17, 1919; New Mexico, January

20, 1919; Nevada, January 21, 1919; Pennsylvania, February 25, 1919; Connecticut, May 6, 1919; New Jersey, March 9, 1922; New York, January 29, 1919; Vermont, January 29, 1919.

xi The Nineteenth Amendment was proposed by Congress on June 4, 1919, when it passed the Senate, Cong. Rec. (66th Cong., 1st Sess.) 635, having previously passed the house on May 21. Id., 94. It appears officially in 41 Stat. 362. Ratification was completed on August 18, 1920, when the thirty-sixth State (Tennessee) approved the amendment, there being then 48 States in the Union. On August 26, 1920, Secretary of Colby certified that it had become a part of the Constitution. 41 Stat. 1823.

The several state legislatures ratified the Nineteenth Amendment on the following dates: Illinois, June 10, 1919 (readopted June 17, 1919); Michigan, June 10, 1919; Wisconsin, June 10, 1919; Kansas, June 16, 1919; New York, June 16, 1919; Ohio, June 16, 1919; Pennsylvania, June 24, 1919; Massachusetts, June 25, 1919; Texas, June 28, 1919; Iowa, July 2, 1919 (date on which approved by Governor); Missouri, July 3, 1919; Arkansas, July 28, 1919; Montana, August 2, 1919 (date on which approved by governor); Nebraska, August 2, 1919; Minnesota, September 8, 1919; New Hampshire, September 10, 1919 (date on which approved by Governor); Utah, October 2, 1919; California, November 1, 1919; Maine, November 5, 1919; North Dakota, December 1, 1919; South Dakota, December 4, 1919 (date on which certified); Colorado, December 15, 1919 (date on which approved by Governor); Kentucky, January 6, 1920; Rhode Island, January 6, 1920; Oregon, January 13, 1920; Indiana, January 16, 1920; Wyoming, January 27, 1920; Nevada, February 7, 1920; New Jersey, February 9, 1920; Idaho, February 11, 1920; Arizona, February 12, 1920; New Mexico, February 21, 1920 (date on which approved by govrnor); Oklahoma, February 28, 1920; West Virginia, March 10, 1920 (confirmed September 21, 1920); Vermont, February 8, 1921. The amendment was rejected by Georgia on July 24, 1919; by Alabama on September 22, 1919; by South Carolina on January 29, 1920; by Virginia on February 12, 1920; by Maryland on February 24, 1920; by Mississippi on March 29, 1920; by Louisiana on July 1, 1920. This amendment was subsequently ratified by Virginia in 1952, Alabama in 1953, Florida in 1969, and Georgia and Louisiana in 1970.

xii The Twentieth Amendment was proposed by Congress on March 2, 1932, when it passed the Senate, Cong. Rec. (72d Cong., 1st Sess.) 5086, having previously passed the House on March 1. Id., 5027. It appears officially in 47 Stat. 745. Ratification was completed on January 23, 1933, when the thirty-sixth State approved the amendment, there being then 48 States in the Union. On February 6, 1933, Secretary of State Stimson certified that it had become a part of the Constitution. 47 Stat. 2569.

The several state legislatures ratified the Twentieth Amendment on the following dates: Virginia, March 4, 1932; New York, March 11, 1932; Mississippi, March 16, 1932; Arkansas March 17, 1932; Kentucky, March 17, 1932; New Jersey, March 21, 1932; South Carolina, March 25, 1932; Michigan, March 31, 1932; Maine, April 1, 1932; Rhode Island, April 14, 1932; Illinois, April 21, 1932; Louisiana, June 22, 1932; West Virginia, July 30, 1932; Pennsylvania, August 11, 1932; Indiana, August 15, 1932; Texas, September 7, 1932; Alabama, September 13, 1932; California, January 4, 1933; North Carolina, January 5, 1933; North Dakota, January 9, 1933; Minnesota, January 12, 1933; Arizona, January 13, 1933; Montana, January 13, 1933; Nebraska, January 13, 1933; Oklahoma, January 13, 1933; Kansas, January 16, 1933; Oregon, January 16, 1933; Delaware, January 19, 1933; Washington, January 19, 1933; Wyoming, January 19, 1933; Iowa, January 20, 1933; South Dakota, January 20, 1933; Tennessee, January 20, 1933; Idaho, January 21, 1933; New Mexico, January 21, 1933; Georgia, January 23, 1933; Missouri, January 23, 1933; Ohio, January 23, 1933; Utah, January 23, 1933; Colorado, January 24, 1933; Massachusetts, January 24, 1933; Wisconsin, January 24, 1933; Nevada, January 26, 1933; Connecticut, January 27, 1933; New Hampshire, January 31, 1933; Vermont, February 2, 1933; Maryland, March 24, 1933; Florida, April 26, 1933.

xiii The Twenty-first Amendment was proposed by Congress on February 20, 1933, when it passed the House, Cong. Rec. (72d Cong., 2d Sess.) 4516, having previously passed the Senate on February 16. Id., 4231. It appears officially in 47 Stat. 1625. Ratification was completed on December 5, 1933, when the thirty-sixth State (Utah) approved the amendment, there being then 48 States in the Union. On December 5, 1933, Acting Secretary of State Phillips certified that it had been adopted by the requisite number of States. 48 Stat. 1749.

The several state conventions ratified the Twenty-first Amendment on the following dates: Michigan, April 10, 1933; Wisconsin, April 25, 1933; Rhode Island, May 8, 1933; Wyoming, May 25, 1933; New

Jersey, June 1, 1933; Delaware, June 24, 1933; Indiana, June 26, 1933; Massachusetts, June 26, 1933; New York, June 27, 1933; Illinois, July 10, 1933; Iowa, July 10, 1933; Connecticut, July 11, 1933; New Hampshire, July 11, 1933; California, July 24, 1933; West Virginia, July 25, 1933; Arkansas, August 1, 1933; Oregon, August 7, 1933; Alabama, August 8, 1933; Tennessee, August 11, 1933; Missouri, August 29, 1933; Arizona, September 5, 1933; Nevada, September 5, 1933; Vermont, September 23, 1933; Colorado, September 26, 1933; Washington, October 3, 1933; Minnesota, October 10, 1933; Idaho, October 17, 1933; Maryland, October 18, 1933; Virginia, October 25, 1933; New Mexico, November 2, 1933; Florida, November 14, 1933; Texas, November 24, 1933; Kentucky, November 27, 1933; Ohio, December 5, 1933; Pennsylvania, December 5, 1933; Utah, December 5, 1933; Maine, December 6, 1933; Montana, August 6, 1934. The amendment was rejected by a convention in the State of South Carolina, on December 4, 1933. The electorate of the State of North Carolina voted against holding a convention at a general election held on November 7, 1933.

xiv The Twenty-second Amendment was proposed by Congress on March 24, 1947, having passed the House on March 21, 1947, Cong. Rec. (80th Cong., 1st Sess.) 2392, and having previously passed the Senate on March 12, 1947. Id., 1978. It appears officially in 61 Stat. 959. Ratification was completed on February 27, 1951, when the thirty-sixth State (Minnesota) approved the amendment, there being then 48 States in the Union. On March 1, 1951, Jess Larson, Administrator of General Services, certified that it had been adopted by the requisite number of States. 16 Fed. Reg. 2019.

A total of 41 state legislatures ratified the Twenty-second Amendment on the following dates: Maine, March 31, 1947; Michigan, March 31, 1947; Iowa, April 1, 1947; Kansas, April 1, 1947; New Hampshire, April 1, 1947; Delaware, April 2, 1947; Illinois, April 3, 1947; Oregon, April 3, 1947; Colorado, April 12, 1947; California, April 15, 1947; New Jersey, April 15, 1947; Vermont, April 15, 1947; Ohio, April 16, 1947; Wisconsin, April 16, 1947; Pennsylvania, April 29, 1947; Connecticut, May 21, 1947; Missouri, May 22, 1947; Nebraska, May 23, 1947; Virginia, January 28, 1948; Mississippi, February 12, 1948; New York, March 9, 1948; South Dakota, January 21, 1949; North Dakota, February 25, 1949; Louisiana, May 17, 1950; Montana, January 25, 1951; Indiana, January 29, 1951; Idaho, January 30, 1951; New Mexico, February 12, 1951; Wyoming, February 12, 1951; Arkansas, February 15, 1951; Georgia, February 17, 1951; Tennessee, February 20, 1951; Texas, February 22, 1951; Utah, February 26, 1951; Nevada, February 26, 1951; Minnesota, February 27, 1951; North Carolina, February 28, 1951; South Carolina, March 13, 1951; Maryland, March 14, 1951; Florida, April 16, 1951; and Alabama, May 4, 1951.

xv The Twenty-third Amendment was proposed by Congress on June 16, 1960, when it passed the Senate, Cong. Rec. (86th Cong., 2d Sess.) 12858, having previously passed the House on June 14. Id., 12571. It appears officially in 74 Stat. 1057. Ratification was completed on March 29, 1961, when the thirty-eighth State (Ohio) approved the amendment, there being then 50 States in the Union. On April 3, 1961, John L. Moore, Administrator of General Services, certified that it had been adopted by the requisite number of States. 26 Fed. Reg. 2808.

The several state legislatures ratified the Twenty-third Amendment on the following dates: Hawaii, June 23, 1960; Massachusetts, August 22, 1960; New Jersey, December 19, 1960; New York, January 17, 1961; California, January 19, 1961; Oregon, January 27, 1961; Maryland, January 30, 1961; Idaho, January 31, 1961; Maine, January 31, 1961; Minnesota, January 31, 1961; New Mexico, February 1, 1961; Nevada, February 2, 1961; Montana, February 6, 1961; Colorado, February 8, 1961; Washington, February 9, 1961; West Virginia, February 9, 1961; Alaska, February 10, 1961; Wyoming, February 13, 1961; South Dakota, February 14, 1961; Delaware, February 20, 1961; Utah, February 21, 1961; Wisconsin, February 21, 1961; Pennsylvania, February 28, 1961; Indiana, March 3, 1961; North Dakota, March 3, 1961; Tennessee, March 6, 1961; Michigan, March 8, 1961; Connecticut, March 9, 1961; Arizona, March 10, 1961; Illinois, March 14, 1961; Nebraska, March 15, 1961; Vermont, March 15, 1961; Iowa, March 16, 1961; Missouri, March 20, 1961; Oklahoma, March 21, 1961; Rhode Island, March 22, 1961; Kansas, March 29, 1961; Ohio, March 29, 1961, and New Hampshire, March 30, 1961.

xvi The Twenty-fourth Amendment was proposed by Congress on September 14, 1962, having passed the House on August 27, 1962. Cong. Rec. (87th Cong., 2d Sess.) 17670 and having previously passed the Senate on March 27, 1962. Id., 5105. It appears officially in 76 Stat. 1259. Ratification was completed on January 23, 1964, when the thirty- eighth State (South Dakota) approved the Amendment, there being then 50 States in the Union. On February 4, 1964, Bernard L. Boutin, Administrator of General

Services, certified that it had been adopted by the requisite number of States. 25 Fed. Reg. 1717. President Lyndon B. Johnson signed this certificate.

Thirty-eight state legislatures ratified the Twenty-fourth Amendment on the following dates: Illinois, November 14, 1962; New Jersey, December 3, 1962; Oregon, January 25, 1963; Montana, January 28, 1963; West Virginia, February 1, 1963; New York, February 4, 1963; Maryland, February 6, 1963; California, February 7, 1963; Alaska, February 11, 1963; Rhode Island, February 14, 1963; Indiana, February 19, 1963; Michigan, February 20, 1963; Utah, February 20, 1963; Colorado, February 21, 1963; Minnesota, February 27, 1963; Ohio, February 27, 1963; New Mexico, March 5, 1963; Hawaii, March 6, 1963; North Dakota, March 7, 1963; Idaho, March 8, 1963; Washington, March 14, 1963; Vermont, March 15, 1963; Nevada, March 19, 1963; Connecticut, March 20, 1963; Tennessee, March 21, 1963; Pennsylvania, March 25, 1963; Wisconsin, March 26, 1963; Kansas, March 28, 1963; Massachusetts, March 28, 1963; Nebraska, April 4, 1963; Florida, April 18, 1963; Iowa, April 24, 1963; Delaware, May 1, 1963; Missouri, May 13, 1963; New Hampshire, June 16, 1963; Kentucky, June 27, 1963; Maine, January 16, 1964; South Dakota, January 23, 1964.

[xvii] This Amendment was proposed by the Eighty-ninth Congress by Senate Joint Resolution No. 1, which was approved by the Senate on February 19, 1965, and by the House of Representatives, in amended form, on April 13, 1965. The House of Representatives agreed to a Conference Report on June 30, 1965, and the Senate agreed to the Conference Report on July 6, 1965. It was declared by the Administrator of General Services, on February 23, 1967, to have been ratified.

This Amendment was ratified by the following States: Nebraska, July 12, 1965; Wisconsin, July 13, 1965; Oklahoma, July 16, 1965; Massachusetts, August 9, 1965; Pennsylvania, August 18, 1965; Kentucky, September 15, 1965; Arizona, September 22, 1965; Michigan, October 5, 1965; Indiana, October 20, 1965; California, October 21, 1965; Arkansas, November 4, 1965; New Jersey, November 29, 1965; Delaware, December 7, 1965; Utah, January 17, 1966; West Virginia, January 20, 1966; Maine, January 24, 1966; Rhode Island, January 28, 1966; Colorado, February 3, 1966; New Mexico, February 3, 1966; Kansas, February 8, 1966; Vermont, February 10, 1966; Alaska, February 18, 1966; Idaho, March 2, 1966; Hawaii, March 3, 1966; Virginia, March 8, 1966; Mississippi, March 10, 1966; New York, March 14, 1966; Maryland, March 23, 1966; Missouri, March 30, 1966; New Hampshire, June 13, 1966; Louisiana, July 5, 1966; Tennessee, January 12, 1967; Wyoming, January 25, 1967; Washington, January 26, 1967; Iowa, January 26, 1967; Oregon, February 2, 1967; Minnesota, February 10, 1967; Nevada, February 10, 1967; Connecticut, February 14, 1967; Montana, February 15, 1967; South Dakota, March 6, 1967; Ohio, March 7, 1967; Alabama, March 14, 1967; North Carolina, March 22, 1967 Illinois, March 22, 1967; Texas, April 25, 1967; Florida, May 25, 1967.

Publication of the certifying statement of the Administrator of General Services that the Amendment had become valid was made on February 25, 1967, F.R. Doc. 67-2208, 32 Fed. Reg. 3287.

[xviii] The Twenty-sixth Amendment was proposed by Congress on March 23, 1971, upon passage by the House of Representatives, the Senate having previously passed an identical resolution on March 10, 1971. It appears officially in 85 Stat. 825. Ratification was completed on July 1, 1971, when action by the legislature of the 38th State, North Carolina, was concluded, and the Administrator of the General Services Administration officially certified it to have been duly ratified on July 5, 1971. 36 Fed. Reg. 12725.

As of the publication of this volume, 42 States had ratified this Amendment: Connecticut, March 23, 1971; Delaware, March 23, 1971; Minnesota, March 23, 1971; Tennessee, March 23, 1971; Washington, March 23, 1971; Hawaii, March 24, 1971; Massachusetts, March 24, 1971; Montana, March 29, 1971; Arkansas, March 30, 1971; Idaho, March 30, 1971; Iowa, March 30, 1971; Nebraska, April 2, 1971; New Jersey, April 3, 1971; Kansas, April 7, 1971; Michigan, April 7, 1971; Alaska, April 8, 1971; Maryland, April 8, 1971; Indiana, April 8, 1971; Maine, April 9, 1971; Vermont, April 16, 1971; Louisiana, April 17, 1971; California, April 19, 1971; Colorado, April 27, 1971; Pennsylvania, April 27, 1971; Texas, April 27, 1971; South Carolina, April 28, 1971; West Virginia, April 28, 1971; New Hampshire, May 13, 1971; Arizona, May 14, 1971; Rhode Island, May 27, 1971; New York, June 2, 1971; Oregon, June 4, 1971; Missouri, June 14, 1971; Wisconsin, June 22, 1971; Illinois, June 29, 1971; Alabama, June 30, 1971; Ohio, June 30, 1971; North Carolina, July 1, 1971; Oklahoma, July 1, 1971; Virginia, July 8, 1971; Wyoming, July 8, 1971; Georgia, October 4, 1971.

[xix] This purported amendment was proposed by Congress on September 25, 1789, when it passed the Senate, having previously passed the House on September 24. (1 Annals of Congress 88, 913). It appears officially in 1 Stat. 97. Having received in 1789-1791 only six state ratifications, the proposal then failed of ratification while ten of the 12 sent to the States by Congress were ratified and proclaimed and became the Bill of Rights. The provision was proclaimed as having been ratified and having become the 27th Amendment, when Michigan ratified on May 7, 1992, there being 50 States in the Union. Proclamation was by the Archivist of the United States, pursuant to 1 U.S.C. Sec. 106b, on May 19, 1992. F.R.Doc. 92-11951, 57 Fed. Reg. 21187. It was also proclaimed by votes of the Senate and House of Representatives. 138 Cong. Rec. (daily ed) S 6948-49, H 3505-06.

The several state legislatures ratified the proposal on the following dates: Maryland, December 19, 1789; North Carolina, December 22, 1789; South Carolina, January 19, 1790; Delaware, January 28, 1790; Vermont, November 3, 1791; Virginia, December 15, 1791; Ohio, May 6, 1873; Wyoming, March 6, 1978; Maine, April 27, 1983; Colorado, April 22, 1984; South Dakota, February 1985; New Hampshire, March 7, 1985; Arizona, April 3, 1985; Tennessee, May 28, 1985; Oklahoma, July 10, 1985; New Mexico, February 14, 1986; Indiana, February 24, 1986; Utah, February 25, 1986; Arkansas, March 13, 1987; Montana, March 17, 1987; Connecticut, May 13, 1987; Wisconsin, July 15, 1987; Georgia, February 2, 1988; West Virginia, March 10, 1988; Louisiana, July 7, 1988; Iowa, February 9, 1989; Idaho, March 23, 1989; Nevada, April 26, 1989; Alaska, May 6, 1989; Oregon, May 19, 1989; Minnesota, May 22, 1989; Texas, May 25, 1989; Kansas, April 5, 1990; Florida, May 31, 1990; North Dakota, Mary 25, 1991; Alabama, May 5, 1992; Missouri, May 5, 1992; Michigan, May 7, 1992. New Jersey subsequently ratified on May 7, 1992.

AUTHORS

 **Attorney David C. Gibbs III** is the President and General Counsel of the National Center for Life and Liberty, a ministry organization that defends life and liberty freedoms nationwide. Mr. Gibbs speaks regularly to audiences in churches and conferences while also litigating cases as a trial attorney. He hosts the weekly radio programs *Law Talk Live*, *Law Talk 5*, and *Law Talk Weekend* and has authored five books including *Fighting for Dear Life* and *Understanding the Constitution*.

Attorney Gibbs graduated from Duke Law School and manages the Gibbs Law Firm with offices in Dallas, Texas; St. Petersburg, Florida; and Washington, D.C. He is admitted to practice before the United States Supreme Court and numerous federal circuit and district courts nationwide. He has also been admitted to the State Bars of Florida, Minnesota, Colorado, North Dakota, Ohio, Texas, Tennessee, Michigan, and the District of Columbia.

Attorney Gibbs was the lead attorney in the Terri Schiavo case representing the parents as they fought to save the life of their daughter. This case went before the United States Supreme Court twice in ten days. Mr. Gibbs is a frequent spokesperson on radio and television having appeared on many major news and talk programs.

 Attorney Barbara J. Weller has been with Gibbs Law Firm for more than twenty years. Her specialty is Constitutional Law, focusing on the Founding Era, life issues, and First Amendment issues, including religious liberty and free speech. She graduated from Regent University School of Law in Virginia Beach, Virginia, where she served as Editor-in-Chief of the Regent Law Review. In addition to her law degree, she has a B.A. in history from Albright College in Reading, Pennsylvania and a Master's Degree in Old Testament studies from Biblical Theological Seminary in Hatfield, Pennsylvania. She also studied at McGill University in Montreal, Canada, at Eastern Baptist Theological Seminary, and at Heidelberg College in Tiffin, Ohio.